Legal Agreements in Plain English

Joel D. Joseph, J.D. and Jeffrey Hiller, J.D.

Contemporary Books, Inc.
Chicago

Library of Congress Cataloging in Publication Data

Joseph, Joel D.
Legal agreements in plain English.

Includes index.
1. Contracts—United States—Language. 2. Contracts—United States—Forms. I. Hiller, Jeffrey. II. Title.
KF801.Z9J67 346.73'02 81-69609
ISBN 0-8092-5811 (pbk.) 347.3062 AACR2

The forms used in this book have been modified from standard forms used by lawyers. Very few legal forms have been approved as a whole by courts of law because a good form is not usually the subject of litigation.

It has been noted that a good agreement can be understood by a non-lawyer of reasonable intelligence. Before signing any legal agreement make sure that you understand it. If you have any doubts about the meaning or effect of an agreement consult an attorney in your jurisdiction.

Published by Contemporary Books, Inc.
180 North Michigan Avenue, Chicago, Illinois 60601
Manufactured in the United States of America
Library of Congress Catalog Card Number: 81-69609
International Standard Book Number: 0-8092-5811-0

Published simultaneously in Canada by
Beaverbooks, Ltd.
150 Lesmill Road
Don Mills, Ontario M3B 2T5
Canada

Joel Joseph: In memory of my mother, Doris Joseph, whose persistent corrections improved my grammar, and whose principles of justice I use as my guide.

Jeffrey Hiller: In memory of my father, Sidney Lipps; to my mother, Beverly Lipps; to my grandmother, Edith Teich; and especially to Laurie Londoner.

Contents

Forms

Preface

Legal agreements are not the most exciting aspect of our lives, but no one can dispute their importance. One *can,* however, dispute the confusing and bulky language in which contracts are usually written. It creates a headache and an unnecessary burden for the average person who wants to conduct a simple business transaction but is forced to wade through waist-deep legalese to do so.

We are lawyers, and we confront this complex dialect every day. In fact, legal language is expected to flow from our lips; instead we find ourselves constantly looking for simple, clear-cut contracts for our clients. When a search of the bookstores showed the absence of a handy book of agreements with simple explanations, we decided to write one to fulfill this need.

Our purpose in this book is to provide the nonlawyer with some principles, definitions, and forms with which to conduct basic legal business.

A word here about pronouns: we have constructed this book as simply as possible, and sometimes the gymnastics of constructing sexually neutral he/she, his/her clauses can obscure the basic clarity of an otherwise simple sentence. So, let it be known that we have no desire to offend anyone in dispensing with this cumbersome style; in the interest of simplicity we have allowed *he* and *him* to represent all humans, whatever their sex, color, or creed.

Also in the interest of simplicity, we have set the book up so that the explanations and descriptions form the body of each chapter. The forms relating to the text material are at the end of each chapter.

Obviously, this book will not take the place of a lawyer. We encourage you to consult a lawyer when necessary, and we have included a chapter to help you discern when one is needed. This book will help when you do visit a lawyer by clarifying what your needs and concerns will be in various situations. Used as a reference and handbook, it will assist you in a variety of circumstances and business plans without confusing you in the process.

Joel D. Joseph
Jeffrey Hiller

1

Introduction to Basic Legal Agreements

We make legal agreements every day of our lives. When you drive into a gas station and say "Five dollars worth of premium, please," you are making a contract, or an agreement, with the gas station attendant to purchase gasoline.

There are certain essential elements in every contract. We will use the term *contract* synonymously with *agreement*. Every contract must have the following elements:

1. offer
2. acceptance
3. valuable consideration

An *offer* is the offer of money or some other thing of value in exchange for an item or service. Example: "I will pay you $50 for that bicycle."

To become an agreement or a contract, the offer must be accepted. When you are shopping to purchase a home, a real estate agent may ask you to fill out a contract form stating the price that you will offer for the home. When you fill out a form such as that, you are making an offer. If the current owner of the home accepts the offer, you have a legally binding contract.

The owner of the home may reject your offer and ask that you pay more for the home. This would be a new offer, or what is known as a *counteroffer*.

To make the offer and the acceptance into a contract there must be valuable consideration. Each person must put up something of value, which may be a promise to pay a certain amount of money or to perform services. A single dollar is usually enough consideration to validate a contract.

To avoid misunderstandings in contracts, the following practices are usually a good idea:

Put it in writing

A contract can be verbal or written. Certain contracts must be written, a contract to buy a home, for example. Putting your agreements into writing minimizes the likelihood of a dispute. Other lawyers may hate us for saying this, but thousands of lawsuits can be avoided by making agreements in the form of clear, understandable, written documents.

Keep a copy; get a receipt

Whenever you sign anything, make sure that you get a copy of it. Whenever you pay for anything, make certain that you get a receipt. If you pay by check, your canceled check is your receipt.

Sign every page of the agreement

Every page of every form in this book has signature lines. In a multipage agreement, if you sign only the last page, changes can be made on the other pages or additional pages can be inserted after you sign, possibly binding you to a contract substantially different from the agreement you intended to make.

Our intention in this book is to offer an alternative to the confusing legal terms and excess verbal baggage that characterize most legal documents. A contract does not have to be stuffed with multisyllabic words such as *hereinafter, whereas, witnesseth, party of the first part, party of the second part, hereinto,* and *to wit* to be valid. Obviously, the most important consideration in an agreement is that everyone signing it fully understands what it means. To achieve that end, we have carefully removed the confusing terms from all the forms in this book.

Contracts with Minors

A contract with a minor is generally unenforceable. For example, if you sell a stereo system to a fourteen-year-old for $50, and he returns it to you battered beyond recognition and demands his money back, you may be forced to reimburse him because the contract was considered against public policy. The definition of a minor varies from state to state, but eighteen is usually the youngest age of adulthood. Every state recognizes the rights of persons twenty-one and over to enter into contracts. Therefore, when negotiating with someone under age twenty-one, check with a local attorney to find out the law in your state regarding minors.

Modifications to Contracts

The contracts included in this book can be modified to suit your specific needs. They provide a basic structure for your agreement but can be changed to conform to your purposes.

Any contract that can be made can be changed. If everyone involved in the contract agrees, a new contract can be substituted for the old one, or the contract can be revoked. However, it is a different story when a contract is breached, or broken. See Chapter 12 for information on dealing with this situation.

2

Love and Marriage

Palimony has recently become a household word. In the United States millions of couples are living together without the benefit or disadvantage of marriage. Actor Lee Marvin was sued by his live-in girlfriend for support, alimony, and property. This has alarmed many couples who have been living together without being married.

The courts will generally recognize as valid agreements and contracts those which are entered into freely between two or more adults. Many individuals desire to settle their property rights before they live together so that they will each know their commitments, obligations, and responsibilities. This is also true for individuals who are getting married and want to settle their property rights prior to their marriage.

With all of the agreements discussed in this chapter, and in this book in general, you can add and eliminate paragraphs to conform to your specific needs.

Premarriage, or prenuptial, agreements are agreements to modify marital property rights before the marriage. Form 1 is this type of agreement, as it defines the intent of the couple to continue to be treated as if they were single even after they are married. In this agreement the future husband and wife both agree to give up any claim to alimony payments or to the property of the other spouse. In other words, if Mr. A owns a home prior to marriage to Ms. B, who owns a boat, this agreement would allow each to continue to be the sole owner of that property. In the event of divorce the property would remain with the original owner.

The couple should list the specific items that each owns prior to marriage and attach the list to the premarriage agreement.

Form 2 is a mutual release regarding living together, or a *palimony agreement*. This form is used to prevent future support and property obligations that may arise when a couple decides to live together without the benefit, or the detriment, of wedlock.

An agreement to live together provides a more permanent arrangement than a palimony agreement but does not include all the legal entanglements of a traditional marriage. The couple who wants to pool resources without getting married can use Form 3.

Whichever agreement or modified agreement you want to use would probably be upheld by the courts if both of you, freely and voluntarily, agree to the terms of the contract.

When a married couple decides to separate, it is advantageous to both husband and wife to write a separation agreement. Form 4 is a separation agreement for couples without children, which defines property and other rights of the couple but excludes alimony payments.

Separations are more complicated when a married couple has children. In addition to a property settlement, Form 5 specifies which person gets custody of the children and provides for child support payments.

If you and your spouse want an uncontested divorce, you may be able to work out your own property settlement without the assistance of lawyers. An uncontested divorce is a divorce in which neither individual chooses to object to any aspects of the divorce.

When we have clients who are seeking an uncontested divorce, we suggest that they first try to work out a settlement between themselves, rather than hiring lawyers to fight over the property. In coming to a settlement, both sides must determine what they are willing to give up. You must realize that in all probability no one is going to be completely happy with the outcome; you must be prepared to compromise to reach a peaceful agreement.

If it does become necessary for the attorneys or the court to settle property rights, the outcome will be far more uncertain and it is very possible that both sides might end up with substantially less than they originally thought possible. Because of this, as well as because of the legal hassle involved, we try to encourage both partners to try to work out a settlement agreement on their own.

For example, in one case we suggested that the husband and wife try to work out their property settlement themselves. We told them to come back to our office in two days. After reaching a compromise agreement they returned, had it written up, and signed it. Neither of them was particularly joyous about the settlement, but to an objective observer it was obviously fair. If this couple had let attorneys work out the agreement, it would have taken far longer than two days, and the legal fees would have been considerably higher than they were.

If you do reach a settlement, you can take all of your terms to your attorney and have written an agreement that is similar to Forms 4 and 5 at a much less expensive rate than if the lawyer had done this work.

If you and your spouse are unable to agree to property settlement, *then* you can put your attorneys to work, and you really have not lost anything.

In the area of domestic relations, we suggest that you participate as much as possible throughout the entire process. Never be afraid to ask your attorney questions. If you are acting as your own attorney, the most valuable source of information can be the domestic relations law clerk at the court. The clerk can generally tell you everything you need to do to file a proper settlement agreement or divorce. Once a divorce is filed it is generally a matter of public record, so you can ask the clerk if you can see a case in the court files that is similar to yours. You can copy or use provisions from any public complaint; it will not be plagiarism since it is a matter of public record.

Finally, as you know, many divorces are much more complicated than the procedures described above. In these more complex matters, work out as many provisions of your agreement as you can; then see an attorney so that he can make sure that everything is in accordance with local rules and proceed on the complex, non-layman matters.

Form 1

Premarriage Agreement of ____________________ and ____________________

This agreement was entered into on the ____ day of ____________________, 19____, between ____________________ and ____________________. ____________________ and ____________________ contemplate legal marriage under the laws of the state of ____________________. It is their mutual desire to enter into this agreement so that they will continue to control their own property. ____________________ and ____________________ are getting married because of their love for each other and do not desire that their financial interests be changed by their marriage. It is agreed as follows:

1. All property which belongs to ____________________ and ____________________ shall be, and forever remain, the personal estate of him or her, including all interest, rents, and profits which may accrue from this property.

2. ____________________ and ____________________ shall have at all times the full right and authority, in all respects the same as each would have if not married, to use, enjoy, manage and convey all property as may belong to him or her;

PAGE ONE APPROVAL:

____

____

3. ______________________________ and

______________________________ each may make any disposition of his or her property by sale, gift or will during his or her lifetime as each sees fit; and

4. ______________________________ and

______________________________, in the event of a separation or divorce, shall have no right against each other by way of claims for support, alimony, or division of property.

____
MAN

____
WOMAN

Form 2

Mutual Release Regarding Living Together

1. *Parties.* This mutual release agreement is entered into this ____ day of ________________, 19____, by ________________________ and ________________________.

2. *Relationship.* We want to live together, but do not want to acquire any rights or obligations with respect to property, income, or support that might otherwise come to either of us by reason of this temporary union.

3. *Terms of Release.* We give our mutual and complete releases to each other. We waive all rights or interest in the property or income of the other that might in any way arise because of our relationship or rendition of services to each other. We specifically waive all rights to support and maintenance that may arise from our association.

____
MAN

____
WOMAN

Agreement to Live Together

1. *Parties.* This agreement is made this ____ day of ______________________, 19____, by ______________________________ and ______________________________ who presently reside in the state of ______________________.

2. *Relationship.* We wish to live together in a relationship similar to matrimony but do not wish to be bound by the statutory or case-law provisions relating to marriage.

3. *Duration of Relationship.* It is agreed that we will live together for an indefinite period of time subject to the following terms:

4. *Partnership.* We agree that we are a partnership for all purposes;

5. *Common Property.* Any real or personal property acquired during the relationship shall be considered to be owned equally;

6. *Income.* All income of either of us and all our accumulations during the existence of our relationship shall be one fund. Our debts and expenses arising during the existence of our union shall be paid out of this fund. Each of us shall have an equal interest in this sum, an equal right to its management and control, and an equal entitlement to the excess remaining after payment of all debts and expenses;

PAGE ONE APPROVAL:

____

____

7. *Abortion.* If the man desires the abortion of any embryo created by us but the woman wants to bear the child, the woman releases the man from any and all legal obligations of any nature that he might otherwise have by reason of the birth of such a child; and the man must express his disapproval of the birth in writing, signed and notarized and given to the woman at least five months before the birth. The woman shall have the exclusive right to determine whether or not she may have an abortion.

8. *Children.* Any children born of us shall have the surname ______________________________. If both of us want to have, and do have a child by our union, the child shall be maintained and supported from our common fund for as long as we live together. We are equally obligated for the support of the child upon termination of our relationship. We shall, upon termination, be equally obligated to spend not less than one-fifth of our respective incomes for the maintenance and education of the child until he/she reaches the age of eighteen.

9. *Child Custody.* Both of us shall have joint custody of any children. The ________________________ shall have their care and
(MOTHER OR FATHER)
control unless otherwise agreed.

PAGE TWO APPROVAL:

____
MAN

____
WOMAN

10. *Separate property.* All property listed on the pages attached is made a part of this agreement by this reference. The property belongs to the one under whose name it is listed prior to the making of this agreement. All listed property is and shall continue to be the separate property of the person who now owns it. All property received by either or us by gift or inheritance during our relationship shall be the separate property of the one who receives it.

11. *Termination.* Our relationship may be terminated at the sole will and decision of either of us, expressed by a written notice given to the other.

12. *Modification of This Agreement.* This agreement may be modified by any agreement in writing signed by both parties, with one exception: no modifications may decrease the obligations that we have agreed to undertake regarding any children born of our union.

13. *Breach of Contract.* If either party fails to perform any obligations required by this agreement, that one shall be responsible for all legal expenses incurred by the other in obtaining the performance of those obligations, including those incurred in seeking damages for the breach of this agreement.

14. *Application of Law.* The validity of this agreement shall be determined solely under the laws of the state of ____________________ as they may from time to time be changed.

SIGNED:

____
MAN

____
WOMAN

Form 4

Separation Agreement (No Children)

1. *Parties to Agreement.* This agreement is made between

______________________________ (husband), who resides at

____ and

______________________________ (wife), who resides at

____.

2. *Date of Marriage.* The parties were married on

________________________ in the state of ____________________.

3. *Reasons for Separation.* Because of irreconcilable differences, the parties separated on ________________________ and have been living apart since that date.

4. *Children of Marriage.* No children were born of this marriage.

5. *Conduct of the Parties.* The parties may and shall continue to live apart for the rest of their lives. Each shall be free from interference, direct or indirect, by the other as fully as though unmarried. Each may, for his or her separate benefit, engage in any employment, business, or profession that he or she may choose. The parties shall not molest or bother each other.

PAGE ONE APPROVAL:

____

____

6. *Property Settlement.* The parties have divided their property to their mutual satisfaction as follows:

____

____

____

____

7. *Debts.* Husband and wife agree that they are no longer liable for the debts of the other and will take reasonable steps to prevent the other from being billed for his or her debts.

8. *Alimony.* The parties agree that neither of them shall be required to provide alimony or support payment to the other. The parties further agree that neither of them shall have the right to seek alimony or support in any court.

____
MAN

____
WOMAN

Separation Agreement (Children)

1. *Parties to Agreement.* This agreement is made between

______________________ (husband), who resides at

______________________ and

______________________ (wife), who resides at

______________________.

2. *Date of Marriage.* The parties were married on

______________________ in the state of ______________________.

3. *Reasons for Separation.* Because of irreconcilable differences, the parties separated on ______________________ and have been living apart since that date.

4. *Children of Marriage.* The following children were born of this marriage.

NAME:	DATE OF BIRTH:
______________________	______________________
______________________	______________________
______________________	______________________

5. *Conduct of the Parties.* The parties may and shall continue to live apart for the rest of their lives. Each shall be free from interference, direct or indirect, by the other as fully as though umarried. Each may, for his or her separate benefit, engage in any employment, business, or profession that he or she may choose. The parties shall not molest or malign each other.

PAGE ONE APPROVAL:

____

MAN

____

WOMAN

6. *Property Settlement.* The parties have divided their property to their mutual satisfaction as follows: ______________________

____

____

____

____

7. *Debts.* Husband and wife agree that they are no longer liable for the debts of the other and will take reasonable steps to prevent the other from being billed for his or her debts.

8. *Alimony.* The parties agree that neither of them shall be required to provide alimony or support payments to the other. The parties further agree that neither of them shall have the right to seek alimony or support in any court.

9. *Custody of Children.* The mother shall have custody of

____

The father shall have custody of

____

10. *Child Support.* The ________________ shall pay the ________________ the sum of $ _________ for child support, per child, on the first day of every month until each child reaches the age of eighteen. These payments shall be increased every July, by the percentage increase in the cost of living as measured by the Consumer Price Index for consumer goods for the previous year.

____

MAN

____

WOMAN

3

Wheels, Etc.

Are you selling your car, boat, airplane, bicycle, moped, or unicycle? We get many calls from clients who want to sell a vehicle, asking if they should have a contract. Our answer is always an emphatic "yes," since problems can often arise in any sale entered into without a written agreement. For example, one of our clients sold a used car, and about two days later the car developed every mechanical problem possible. Our client was sued by the buyer for knowingly selling a defective car and for breach of warranty. After several conferences the case was settled by refunding $200 of the purchase price to the buyer, and our client was charged $300 in legal fees. This case easily could have been avoided.

Whenever you are selling a used car or other personal property, you should have a contract.

Contract for Sale of a Vehicle

If you are the seller, you should limit your liability by selling the personal property *as is*, which means that you are making no representations as to the condition of the property. Once the seller conveys the property sold in *as is* condition and receives payment, he is generally not liable for anything that happens to the property after it has been delivered to the buyer.

A contract for sale of a vehicle is recommended when you sell your car or truck. Form 6 is a contract for sale of a vehicle which describes the vehicle in detail by serial number and body style. This agreement does not include a mechanical warranty, so the car is sold as is—what you see is what you get—with no warranties being expressed concerning mechanical condition of the vehicle.

Form 6 is designed to eliminate the problems discussed previously. The provision entitled "Warranty of Title" means that the seller of the vehicle owns the property outright that he is selling. You cannot sell something you do not own; this particular paragraph simply states that you own the property and will defend your ownership against anyone else who might come along and claim ownership.

Once this contract is signed by both parties and the property is exchanged, the seller is no longer responsible for the condition or repair of the property.

Buyer Beware!

Before buying a used car, check it out thoroughly. Either take a mechanic with you to inspect the vehicle or take the car to the mechanic before signing a contract to buy it. If the seller won't let you have a mechanic inspect the car, don't buy it unless the price is low enough to make it a good purchase even if it needs a new engine and transmission.

If you buy a used car from a used car dealer, you may get a thirty- or ninety-day warranty. You will probably pay more for a used car from a dealer than from an individual, so shop around. Don't buy the first car that you see.

Ask questions. Is the owner the original owner? Does the owner have a complete service record for the vehicle? Is the odometer mileage accurate? Does the car use much oil? How much? Was the car ever in an accident? If the owner lies to you in answering these questions, you may be able to sue him for fraud.

SELLER BEWARE!

Tell the truth about your car. Show the potential buyer the service records. If you intentionally mislead the buyer about the car, or set the odometer back, the buyer can sue you for fraud. You are not required to volunteer every negative fact or thought about the car, but if you are asked, you must supply accurate information.

BILL OF SALE

A bill of sale is often needed by a department of motor vehicles in the state where the buyer wants the vehicle to be licensed. Form 7 is a bill of sale that meets the requirements of motor vehicle departments for licensing. This is useful for two purposes. First, it limits the liability of the seller; the seller is merely saying, "I own the automobile and no one else has a claim of ownership." Second, this bill of sale, showing the purchase price, may be presented by the buyer to a department of motor vehicles for sales tax and ownership purposes. This bill of sale says nothing about the condition of the vehicle for the reasons discussed above. The bill of sale is also useful as a receipt.

We suggest that you use Forms 6 and 7 together if you are selling or buying a vehicle or other personal property. This will define your liability, as well as provide a receipt for proof of purchase. The receipt comes in especially handy regarding taxes—if you do not have a receipt, some states will decide for themselves how much the vehicle is worth. If you happened to make a good deal on the vehicle and did not have a bill of sale or receipt, you would end up paying more tax than you should, simply because you had no proof of how much money you actually paid.

TRANSFERRING TITLE

Most titles to automobiles have an assignment form on the back. An assignment of the title is required for a new title to be issued. Form 8 is a standard assignment of title used by most states. Use this form if your title does not include an assignment provision.

When you buy or sell a vehicle you should be sure that the title, as well as the vehicle, is properly transferred. While state law may vary, the title must generally include the selling price, the name of the purchaser, and the name of the seller, and it must be witnessed by a notary.

Lease of a Vehicle

Leasing a vehicle has many advantages as well as disadvantages. There may be a tax savings and a deposit when you lease rather than purchase, but to get a clear picture of a leasing arrangement you should consult an attorney or accountant.

Leasing may sound attractive if you have a second car that you are not using and you want to lease it to make some extra money. However, we strongly recommend against privately leasing an automobile. If you lease your automobile, you can be held responsible for the acts of the person to whom you leased the car. If the lessee (the one who leases the car) has an accident in the car, the victim of the accident could sue the lessor (the one who owns the car), because the owner is legally responsible for the property. The small amount of money you might make in leasing would not be worth the risk of being responsible for the potentially wild actions of another person. Even if you buy insurance, you are still subject to additional liability, and the cost of insurance would reduce any potential profit. Unless you go into the leasing business, leasing your private car is not a particularly carefree way to make money.

Sale of Personal Property

Much of what has been said about the sale of a vehicle pertains to the sale of any type of personal property. As you know, a major theme of this book is our belief that it is always advisable to have a written contract. This, of course, applies to personal property as well as everything else. For our purposes, *personal property* will mean all property other than real estate.

Writing a contract for the sale of personal property is advisable when selling items worth more than $100. This type of contract is also important when selling mechanical or electrical items, such as tools or stereo equipment, even if they are sold for less than $100, because of possible repair problems. Form 9 is a contract for sale of personal property that includes no mechanical warranty.

A bill of sale is a receipt that may be useful at tax time. In states that have a personal property tax, a bill of sale will establish the taxable value of the property. Form 10 is a bill of sale that can be used for these purposes; it also includes a warranty that the seller is the true owner of the article.

We again suggest that you sell the property as is. One of our clients had a garage sale. A woman bought a stereo; she took it home and later threatened to sue because after a few uses the stereo didn't work properly. Rather than fighting about it and going to court, our client gave the purchaser her money back. If the seller had had a contract for sale of personal property, she would have been protected and would not have had to refund the money. *Conclusion:* always put your agreements in writing.

Contract for Sale of Vehicle (No Mechanical Warranty)

1. *Buyer and Seller.* ______________________________ (seller) sells and delivers the vehicle described in Paragraph 2 to ______________________________ (buyer).

2. *Description of Vehicle.* The vehicle being sold and delivered by this contract is described as follows:

Make: ______________________________

Serial Number: ______________________________

Body Type: ______________________________

Year Manufactured: ______________________________

3. *Price.* ______________________________ (buyer) agrees to pay ______________________________ (seller) the sum of $ __________ for the vehicle described in Paragraph 2.

4. *Warranty of Title.* Seller warrants that he (she) is the legal owner of this vehicle, that the vehicle is free from all claims, that he (she) has the right to sell this vehicle and he (she) warrants and will defend the title, in court if necessary, against claims of any person.

5. *Mechanical Warranty.* The vehicle is sold in "as is" condition. The seller makes no warranties as to the condition of this vehicle.

____
SELLER DATE

____
BUYER DATE

Form 7

Bill of Sale for Vehicle

In exchange for $ ________, receipt of which is acknowledged by this Bill of Sale, ________________________ (seller) sells and delivers to ________________________ (buyer) the following vehicle:

Make: ____

Serial Number: ______________________________________

Body Type: ____

Year Manufactured: ___________________________________

Seller warrants that he (she) is the legal owner of this vehicle, that the vehicle is free from all claims, that he (she) has the right to sell this vehicle, and he (she) warrants and will defend the title, in court if necessary, against claims of any person.

____
DATE

____
SELLER

Form 8

Assignment of Title

Selling Price $ ________

For value received the undersigned hereby sell(s), assign(s), or transfer(s)

UNTO (Name of purchaser) ______________________________

ADDRESS ______________________________________

(Number) (Street) (Section) (Apt. No.)

the motor vehicle or trailer described on the reverse side of this certificate, and the undersigned hereby warrant(s) the title to said motor vehicle or trailer and certifies that at the time of delivery the same is subject to the following liens or encumbrances and none other:

AMOUNT	KIND	DATE	FAVOR OF

Signature of assigner (seller) ______________________________

On this ____ day of ________________, 19____, before me, the subscriber, a Notary Public of ______________________

personally appeared ____________________ who made oath in due form of law that the above statements are true.

Witness my hand and notarial seal

_________________________, *Notary Public.*

My commission expires: ______________________.

Contract for Sale of Personal Property

1. *Buyer and Seller.* ______________________________ (seller) sells and delivers the personal property described in Paragraph 2 to ______________________________ (buyer).

2. *Description of Personal Property.* The property being sold and delivered by this contract is described as follows:

Make: ______________________________

Serial Number: ______________________________

Description: ______________________________

Year Manufactured: ______________________________

3. *Price.* ______________________________ (buyer) agrees to pay ______________________________ (seller) the sum of $ __________ for the item described in Paragraph 2.

4. *Warranty of Title.* Seller warrants that he/she is the legal owner of this property, that the property is free from all claims, that he/she has the right to sell this property and he/she warrants and will defend the title, in court if necessary, against the claims of any person.

5. *Mechanical Warranty.* This property is sold in "as is" condition. The seller makes no warranties as to the condition of this property.

____
SELLER DATE

____
BUYER DATE

Bill of Sale for Personal Property

In exchange for $ _________, receipt of which is acknowledged by this bill of sale, ______________________________ (seller) sells and delivers to ______________________________ (buyer) the following personal property:

Make: ______________________________

Serial Number: ______________________________

Description: ______________________________

Year Manufactured: ______________________________

Seller warrants that he/she is the legal owner of this property, that the property is free from all claims, that he/she has the right to sell the property, and he/she warrants and will defend the title, in court if necessary, against the claims of any person.

____
DATE

____
SELLER

4

Your Home

You find your dream home—or, more likely, your dream condominium. The real estate agent senses that you love the property and pressures you to sign a contract right then and there. Resist the pressure.

Instead of signing a contract to buy a home, you may want to lease the property with an option to buy. Or you may want to buy an option to buy the property without a lease. Be aware of these choices.

If you think that you want to buy, talk to your attorney first, so he or she can review the contract of sale of the real property. Real property, or real estate, means land or buildings connected to land and includes homes and condominiums.

If you decide not to hire an attorney, carefully read the contract of sale. Make certain that it contains the contingencies needed to protect your rights. A *contingency* is a provision in a contract that provides for the possibility of terminating the contract. Three important contingencies should be included in most contracts to buy real property:

1. financing contingency
2. inspection contingency
3. contingency concerning sale of other property

These contingencies are discussed in more detail in this chapter. Be aware of what they mean.

This chapter will help you understand what your choices are when you are looking to buy a piece of property. If you are selling your home, this chapter will explain the types of agreements that you can have with a real estate broker. It will also help you sell your home without a real estate broker by providing a form for the contract of sale and by explaining real estate terms.

Contract for Sale of Real Property

The purchase of a home is usually the largest transaction that an individual enters into. The contract for sale of real property is the most important document that is signed concerning the purchase or sale of real estate. Most major lawsuits concerning real estate transactions deal with interpretations of the contract for sale. Form 11 is a contract for the sale of real estate that defines the rights and obligations of the purchaser and seller.

Most buyers do not obtain an attorney until after they sign a contract for sale. Real estate brokers convince many purchasers that they must sign a contract on a house or condominium quickly or it will be lost to someone else.

When looking at a home or condominium, make sure that you understand the important elements that should be in your contract of sale. If you intend to hire an attorney, do so *before* you sign the contract on the dotted line.

What Is Included in the Sale?

Make sure that you know, and can point to in the contract, the exact extent of the property that you are buying. Are the blue drapes in the living room included? Is the dining room fixture included? These items are called fixtures, or those items that are physically connected to the home or condominium. Generally, fixtures are included in the sale of real estate, but it is recommended that all items be listed specifically as either included or excluded.

Attorneys make mistakes. We know of one attorney who bought a home and *thought* that he bought a television antenna with it. Under the law he did buy the antenna. However, the seller was unaware of the law and removed the valuable antenna just before the closing, or settlement, took place. Closing, or settlement, is the time that the title to the property legally changes hands; all money is paid and documents are signed at that time.

In the antenna example, the closing could have been called off because the antenna was removed. The buyer could have sued the seller for the value of the antenna, but the legal hassles involved in either alternative just weren't worth the price of a TV antenna. *Conclusion:* make certain that both the buyer and the seller know which items are included in the sale and which aren't by listing them on a separate schedule attached to the contract of sale and referred to in the contract of sale. See Schedule A of Form 11.

Your Old House

Unless you are a multimillionaire, you probably need the money from the sale of your current home or condominium to purchase a new home. This is the perennial problem in real estate transactions.

One way to handle this problem is to put a contingency in the contract concerning the sale of your home. This means that unless you sell your current home within a certain period the deal is off. Paragraph 6d of Form 11 provides for this type of contingency. If you need the proceeds from the sale of your current residence to pay for your new home, make sure that the contract you sign has a contingency based on the sale of your old home. If it does not include such a contingency, add one. Note: any addition to a form contract should be signed or initialed by both the buyer and seller. Otherwise, either party could say that the provision was added after the contract was signed.

Hire a Professional to Inspect the Property

Even if the property you want to buy is new, we recommend that you hire a professional to inspect it. You can find one listed in the *Yellow Pages* under "Building Inspection Service." Be prepared to pay at least $100 for this service. For that fee you are entitled to a detailed inspection and written report regarding the structural, electrical, plumbing, insulation, and heating condition of the property.

When the building inspector checks the property, go with him. Make sure that he goes into every part of the home, including the attic and basement. The basement inspection is very important since basement leaks are found in nearly 50 percent of the homes in the United States.

Don't sign a contract to buy a home unless it includes an inspection contingency. Responsible real estate brokers will include an inspection contingency in their contract forms. Paragraph 6b of Form 11 provides for an inspection within ten days of signing the contract of sale.

Financing Contingency

Unless you intend to pay cash for your house, the contract you sign should allow you to get out of the deal if you cannot secure a loan commitment. If you sign a contract without this type of provision, you run the risk of not getting a loan and being sued for breach of contract. Paragraph 6c of Form 11 provides for a financing contingency.

Listing Agreements with Real Estate Broker

You don't have to use a real estate broker to sell your house or condominium. If you hire a real estate broker, you can bargain with him or her over the fee. It is illegal for real estate brokers to fix their fees; they cannot all agree to charge 6 percent. Most brokers will now sell a home for 5 percent or less.

You can agree with a broker that the fee will be a flat rate—$3,000, for example—if the broker sells your house for at least $80,000. The agreement could provide to give the broker a bonus if he sells it for more than $100,000.

There are three types of agreements to list property with a real estate agent:

1. open listing
2. exclusive listing
3. exclusive right of sale

The open listing is the most commonly used of the three. It occurs when an owner lists his property with more than one real estate agent. The first broker to produce a buyer who is ready, willing, and able to buy your home for the price you want is entitled to receive the specified commission. When the sale is completed it is not necessary for the owner to notify the other real estate agents, because the listing is automatically terminated by the sale. We recommend that you notify the other real estate agents as a courtesy to them and to avoid prospective purchasers from coming to your door. Form 12 is an open listing agreement that may be entered into with more than one real estate broker at the same time; whichever broker effects a sale is entitled to the commission.

An exclusive listing agreement, such as Form 13, ties you to one broker, who earns a commission even if another broker effects the sale of the property. This agreement is similar to the open listing agreement, but the differences are important.

With an open listing agreement, two or more brokers will be competing to sell your home. With an exclusive listing, only one broker can sell your home. Since there will be no competition concerning this sale, the exclusive listing agreement should specify that the broker will advertise and take other steps to sell your house. For the right to an exclusive listing agreement, the broker should be willing to commit himself to certain efforts or agree to take a lower commission.

Concerning an exclusive right of sale agreement, such as Form 14, a broker earns a commission even if you sell the home yourself.

Both the exclusive listing and the exclusive right of sale can involve a multiple listing arrangement. The exclusive broker may belong to a multiple listing service, which maintains a computer listing of homes that is available to any broker who is a member of the service. If you have an exclusive listing, and your broker belongs to a multiple listing service, another broker may locate a buyer for you through the service. In this case, the two brokers split the commission. This is their concern and would not affect you; brokers have written agreements to provide for the sharing of commissions in multiple listing arrangements. Multiple listing services are usually beneficial to the seller, as they increase the likelihood of finding a buyer without increasing the commission fee.

We recommend that you avoid entering into an exclusive right of sale agreement, if possible. Under this type of agreement, even if the broker makes little or no effort to sell your house, and you sell it yourself, the broker still has a claim for a commission.

If you do enter into an exclusive right of sale agreement, make it for a short period, such as ninety days. Also, specify in detail the advertising the broker will pay for and the days that the broker will hold an open house.

Leases

Beware of leasing your house. If you lease your house and then want to sell it, it may be very difficult and expensive to evict a tenant who doesn't want to leave. Owners have had to pay tenants thousands of dollars to avoid lengthly court battles, just to get the tenant to leave their own house!

A lease is one type of agreement for which local, city, county, and state regulations are often complicated and confusing. We recommend that you consult an attorney in your area before leasing your home or condominium. A lease, or a rental agreement, establishes a tenant's right to use an apartment for a specified term.

Form 15 is a simple lease agreement that can be used for lease of either a furnished or an unfurnished home or apartment. If you use this form, consult a local attorney. It is usually less expensive for an attorney to revise a lease than to start from scratch to draft a lease or other legal document.

Leases on furnished homes or apartments should contain a detailed inventory of all pots, pans, dishes, sheets, furniture, and other items that are included in the property. Both parties should carefully inspect the inventory items. For example, if a couch is damaged when the initial inventory is taken, its condition should be described in detail. Both parties should sign the inventory.

The final inventory should take place at the end of the lease term. Representatives of both parties should be present. If you are leasing a furnished home or apartment out of town, make sure that the final inventory takes place in your presence or in the presence of a trusted friend.

A client leased a home in Great Britain for nine months. He didn't break or lose any items that were on the initial inventory, but he left the country before the final inventory was taken. The owner conducted the final inventory by herself and proceeded to list many items as damaged or missing. The tenant later received this list and found that his security deposit was used to replace the "missing" and "damaged" items. Because the owner was 4,000 miles away, and because only a few hundred dollars were at stake, we advised the client to drop the matter. A problem like this can be avoided by having your representative present when the final inventory is taken.

A client brought us a lease to review, which had been drafted by lawyers for a large bank. The lease was at least ten pages long, written in detailed legalese. The bank's lease provided that the leased property had to be insured, but no value for the insurance was specified. We suggested that an amount be agreed on for insurance. Had the building burned down, the tenant could have been sued if the insurance was insufficient. But if all parties agree on the amount of the insurance, the tenant has protection. Sometimes lawyers put in so much legal jargon that they forget the essentials.

Subleases

Subleases are very common in college towns and other places where there is a demand for short-term apartments. Most subleases involve furnished apartments. Because of this, make sure that you have an inventory procedure, as discussed above, on leases of furnished property.

Many leases require the landlord to approve of subleases. A sublease is a lease by the tenant to another tenant, or subtenant. If you are entering into a sublease agreement, make sure that you obtain the landlord's consent, if it is needed.

It is usually advisable for the subtenant to make monthly payments directly to the landlord rather than to the tenant. It is not uncommon for a subtenant to be evicted for nonpayment of rent because the tenant failed to pay rent to the landlord. It is no defense to a suit for eviction that the subtenant paid rent to the tenant.

If you are the tenant, it will probably be to your advantage to have the subtenant pay rent to the landlord; it will prevent delays, since the money will go directly to the landlord. However, make sure that the landlord notifies you if the subtenant is not making payments; if the subtenant fails to pay the rent, you should pay it to protect your right to keep the apartment or house.

To avoid problems, make sure that your subtenant is reliable. Check his credit and other references. Require the subtenant to pay you a security deposit of at least one month's rent, plus one month's rent in advance.

Form 16 is a sublease agreement between a tenant and a subtenant, which should be used only with the original landlord's written consent. A sublease is advisable if you intend to be out of town for a short period of time and then intend to return to your home or apartment. If you do not intend to return to your rental unit, you should not enter into a sublease agreement; it may be advisable to instead assign your lease to the new tenant. Or it may be preferable for the new tenant to enter into a new lease directly with the landlord. You should consult with an attorney in your community for advice concerning this type of situation.

Option To Buy

An option is a right given by an owner to another person to purchase (or lease) the property at some time in the future. You can agree with an owner to buy an option for one week or for one year. You have to pay something for this right. The advantage of an option is that it holds the property for you without committing you to buy it.

If a real estate agent is pressuring you to buy a piece of property, you can offer to buy an option to buy the property. For example, if you like a house, but you want more time to think about it, an option will hold the house for you. If you pay the owner $100 for a seven-day option to buy the house, you will have one week to get an appraisal and an inspection, to consult an attorney, or just to think about it, and only $100 will be at risk.

Form 17 is an option to buy agreement. An option to buy gives the prospective purchaser the right to buy a piece of real estate for a fixed price, but does not commit that person to the purchase.

Lease with an Option to Buy (Lease-Purchase)

If you find a house or condominium that you would like to buy, but you cannot afford the down payment, a lease with an option to buy may suit your needs. You may agree with an owner that part, or all, of the rent paid will be applied to the purchase price.

From the owner's point of view, a lease with an option to buy may not be attractive. Both parties must agree to a purchase price when the lease-purchase agreement is signed. In these inflationary times an owner runs a great risk of fixing too low a price. However, if the owner wants to sell but can't, a lease-purchase may be a realistic option.

Form 18, a lease with an option to purchase, gives possession of property to a tenant coupled with the right to buy the property at a fixed price at a later time.

Form 11

Contract for Sale of Real Property

1. *Date.* This contract was entered into on the ____ day of

____________________, 19______.

2. *Parties.* This contract was entered into between

______________________________, seller, and

______________________________, purchaser.

3. *Offer and Acceptance.* The seller agrees to sell the property described in Paragraph 4, and the purchaser agrees to buy this property, according to the terms of this contract.

4. *Property Description.* The property is located at

____

____ .

Schedule A is attached to this agreement and is included as a part of this contract.

5. *Consideration.* Purchaser agrees to pay the seller the sum of

____________________ dollars ($ __________) for the above-described property.

6. *Terms and Conditions.*

a. *Deposit.* The purchaser shall pay the seller a deposit of

____________________ dollars ($ __________) on or before

________________________.

PAGE ONE APPROVAL:

____

SELLER

____

PURCHASER

b. *Inspection contingency.* The purchaser shall be entitled to have a structural and mechanical inspection of the property by an engineer or other expert of his choosing within ten (10) days of the date stated in Paragraph 1. If the inspection, in the opinion of the purchaser, is unsatisfactory, the purchaser shall be entitled to a refund of the deposit and the contract will be terminated after the deposit is refunded.

c. *Financing contingency.* This contract is contingent on the purchaser securing financing at market rates on the above-described property within ____ days. If, after making best efforts to arrange financing, the purchaser has been unable to secure financing, the purchaser shall be entitled to a refund of the deposit and the contract will be terminated after the deposit is refunded.

d. *Sale contingent on sale of purchaser's real property.* This contract is contingent on the sale of the following property, which is owned by the purchaser:

____

____

If, after making best efforts to sell this home for ____ days, the purchaser has been unable to secure a buyer who is ready, willing, and able to pay at least ______________________ dollars ($ ___________) for this property, the purchaser shall be entitled to a refund of the deposit and the contract will be terminated after the deposit is refunded.

7. *Deed.* Seller agrees to convey title free and clear of all claims by a good and sufficient warranty deed.

PAGE TWO APPROVAL:

____
SELLER

____
PURCHASER

8. *Closing Date and Place.* Seller agrees to surrender possession to purchaser on or before ______________________ at

____

(Location of closing)

9. *Witnessed Signatures of All Principals.* This agreement was signed in the presence of the following witnesses:

Witnesses:

____

WITNESS

____

WITNESS

____

SELLER

____

(ADDRESS)

____

WITNESS

____

WITNESS

____

PURCHASER

____

(ADDRESS)

Schedule A

1. Property included in this sale is described as follows:

____

____

2. Property excluded from this sale is described as follows:

____

____

SCHEDULE A APPROVAL:

____

SELLER

____

PURCHASER

Form 12

Open Listing Agreement

1. *Date.* This agreement was signed on the ____ day of ____________________, 19____.

2. *Parties.* ______________________________ (owner) and ______________________________ (real estate broker) agree as follows:

3. *Listing Term.* Owner lists the property described in Paragraph 4, with the real estate broker for a period of ____ days.

4. *Description of Property.* The property to be listed is located at ____; its lot number is ____; its square number is ____.

5. *Commission.* The owner agrees to pay the real estate broker a commission of __________ (use a flat fee or percentage or combination of the two) if the broker finds a purchaser ready, willing, and able to pay at least $ __________ for the property described in Paragraph 4.

6. *Other Sales.* The owner retains the right to sell the property directly with no sales commission, so long as the broker did not find this purchaser. The owner has the right to list the property with other brokers. If a sale is made within ____ months after this agreement terminates to parties found by the real estate agent during the term of this agreement, and whose names have been disclosed to the owner, the owner is required to pay the commission specified above.

PAGE ONE APPROVAL:

____
OWNER

____
REAL ESTATE BROKER

7. *Forfeit of Deposit.* If a deposit of money is forfeited by a purchaser, one-half shall be retained by the broker, providing that this amount does not exceed the commission, and one-half shall be paid to the owner.

8. *Deed.* If the property is sold, the owner agrees to furnish the purchaser with a good and sufficient warranty deed.

AGREED TO:

____
WITNESS

____
WITNESS

____
WITNESS

____
OWNER

____
OWNER

____
BROKER

Exclusive Listing Agreement

1. *Date.* This agreement was signed on the ____ day of ________________, 19____.

2. *Parties.* ________________________ (owner) and ________________________ (real estate broker) agree as follows:

3. *Listing Term.* Owner lists the property described in Paragraph 4, with the real estate broker for a period of ____ days.

4. *Description of Property.* The property to be listed is located at ________________________________; its lot number is ____; its square number is ____.

5. *Commission.* The owner agrees to pay the real estate broker a commission of ________ (use a flat fee or percentage or combination of the two) should the broker or any other broker find a purchaser ready, willing and able to pay at least $ ________ for the property described in Paragraph 4.

6. *Other Sales.* The owner retains the right to sell the property directly with no sales commission, so long as the broker did not find this purchaser. If a sale is made within ____ months after this agreement terminates to parties found by the real estate agent during the term of this agreement, and whose names have been disclosed to the owner, the owner is required to pay the commission specified above.

____
REAL ESTATE BROKER

____
OWNER

7. *Broker's Efforts to Sell Property.* The broker agrees to use best efforts to sell the property and to advertise the property at least ____ times per week in the following newspapers

____

____

for the duration of this agreement.

8. *Forfeit of Deposit.* If a deposit of money is forfeited by a purchaser, one-half shall be retained by the broker, providing that this amount does not exceed the commission, and one-half shall be paid to the owner.

9. *Deed.* If the property is sold, the owner agrees to furnish the purchaser with a good and sufficient warranty deed.

AGREED TO:

____
WITNESS

____
WITNESS

____
OWNER

____
OWNER

____
BROKER

Exclusive Right of Sale

1. *Date.* This agreement was signed on the ____ day of ____________________, 19____.

2. *Parties.* ______________________________ (owner) and ______________________________ (real estate broker) agree as follows:

3. *Listing Term.* Owner lists the property described in Paragraph 4, with the real estate broker for a period of ____ days.

4. *Description of Property.* The property to be listed is located at ____; its lot block number is ____; its square number is ____.

5. *Commission.* The owner agrees to pay the real estate broker a commission of ____________________ (use a flat fee or percentage, or combination of the two) if the property is sold, or a contract of sale signed during the listing term.

6. *Other Sales.* If a sale is made within ____ months after this agreement terminates, to parties found by the real estate agent during the term of this agreement, and whose names have been disclosed to the owner, the owner is required to pay the commission specified above.

7. *Broker's Efforts to Sell Property.* The broker agrees to use best efforts to sell the property and to advertise the property at least ____ times per week in the following newspapers:

____

for the duration of this agreement.

PAGE ONE APPROVAL:

________________________________ ________________________________

OWNER REAL ESTATE BROKER

8. *Forfeit of Deposit.* If a deposit of money is forfeited by a purchaser, one-half shall be retained by the broker, providing that this amount does not exceed the commission, and one-half shall be paid to the owner.

9. *Deed.* If the property is sold, the owner agrees to furnish the purchaser with a good and sufficient warranty deed.

AGREED TO:

____
WITNESS

____
WITNESS

____
WITNESS

____
OWNER

____
OWNER

____
BROKER

Form 15

Lease of Real Property

1. *Date.* This lease agreement was entered into on the ____ day of ____________________, 19____.

2. *Parties:* ______________________________ (owner) and ______________________________ (tenant).

3. *Leased Property.* The owner agrees to lease to the tenant the following property:

4. *Lease Term.* The term of this lease begins on ________________________ and ends on ________________________.

5. *Rent.* The rent for the property is $ __________ per month, payable on the ____ day of every month.

6. *Security Deposit.* The tenant shall deposit with the owner $ __________ before moving into the property, as a security deposit. The owner shall return the deposit to the tenant after the lease term, along with __________% interest per year, so long as the property has not been damaged by the tenant or by the tenant's negligence.

7. *Use of Property.* The property shall be for ____________________

____ and for no other purpose without the written consent of the owner.

8. *Sublease.* The tenant may not sublease the property without the written consent of the owner.

PAGE ONE APPROVAL:

____
OWNER

____
TENANT

9. *Owner's Maintenance Responsibilities.* The owner agrees to maintain ____

____ .

in good repair. The tenant shall give the owner notice of repairs that need to be made.

10. *Tenant's Maintenance Responsibilities.* The tenant agrees to maintain ______________________________ in good repair.

11. *Utilities.* ______________________________ shall be responsible for all utilities, excluding telephone.

12. *Insurance.* The owner agrees to insure the property against all risks.

13. *Inventory.* Attached to this agreement is an inventory of all furniture, dishes, and other items that were in the leased property on ______________________________ (date). A final inventory will be conducted on ______________________________ (date). The tenant agrees to pay fair market value or repair or replace all items that are damaged or missing on the date that the final inventory is taken.

14. *Remedies for Default.* ______________________________

____ .

15. *Termination.* The tenant agrees to vacate the property at the end of the lease term in as good a condition as it is now, excepting ordinary wear and tear.

AGREED TO:

____
TENANT

____
OWNER

Sublease

1. *Parties.* This sublease was entered into between

_____________________ (tenant) and

_____________________ (subtenant).

2. *Sublease Period.* The subtenant agrees to lease

_____________________ (describe property to be leased) from _____________ to _____________.

3. *Terms of Sublease.* The subtenant agrees to comply with all terms and conditions of the lease entered into by the tenant. The lease agreement is incorporated into this agreement by reference. The subtenant agrees to pay the landlord the monthly rent stated in that lease, which is $ _______.

4. *Security Deposit.* The subtenant agrees to pay the tenant the sum of $ _______ as a security deposit.

5. *Consideration.* The subtenant agrees to pay the tenant the sum of $ _______ in consideration of this agreement.

6. *Inventory.* Attached to this agreement is an inventory of items that were in the above-described property on _____________ (date). The subtenant agrees to replace or reimburse the tenant for any of these items that are missing or damaged.

7. *Landlord's Consent.* The landlord consents to this sublease and agrees to promptly notify the tenant at _____________

_____________________ (address) if the subtenant is in breach of this agreement.

____
LANDLORD DATE

____
TENANT DATE

____
SUBTENANT DATE

Form 17

Option to Buy Agreement

1. *Date.* This agreement was entered into on the ____ day of ____________________, 19____.

2. *Parties.* ______________________________ (owner) and ______________________________ (buyer).

3. *Option Terms.* Buyer agrees to pay $ __________ to the owner for the right to buy ____ (description of real property) for $ __________ until ____________ (date).

4. *Exercise of Option.* The buyer must notify the owner in writing during the option period if he or she decides to exercise the option.

If buyer exercises the option, the owner agrees to sign the attached contract of sale. (Attach a contract of sale form, with all blanks filled in.)

AGREED TO:

____
OWNER

____
BUYER

Lease with an Option to Buy (Lease-Purchase)

1. *Date.* This lease agreement was entered into on the ____ day of ____________________, 19____.

2. *Parties:* ________________________________ (owner) and ________________________________ (tenant).

3. *Leased Property.* The owner agrees to lease to the tenant the following property:

____.

4. *Lease Term.* The term of this lease begins on ________________________ and ends on ________________________.

5. *Rent.* The rent for the property is $ __________ per month, payable on the ____ day of every month.

6. *Security Deposit.* The tenant shall deposit with the owner $ __________ before moving into the property, as a security deposit. The owner shall return the deposit to the tenant after the lease term, along with ____% interest per year, so long as the property has not been damaged by the tenant or by the tenant's negligence.

7. *Use of Property.* The property shall be for ____________________ ____ and for no other purpose without the written consent of the owner.

PAGE ONE APPROVAL:

____
OWNER

____
TENANT

8. *Sublease.* The tenant may not sublease the property without the written consent of the owner.

9. *Owner's Maintenance Responsibilities.* The owner agrees to maintain ____

____

in good repair. The tenant shall give the owner notice of repairs that need to be made.

10. *Tenant's Maintenance Responsibilities.* The tenant agrees to maintain ______________________________ in good repair.

11. *Insurance.* The tenant agrees to insure the property against all risks for $ ________.

12. *Remedies for Default.* ______________________________

____.

13. *Termination.* The tenant agrees to vacate the property at the end of the lease term in as good condition as it is now, excepting ordinary wear and tear.

14. *Option Terms.* Tenant has the right to purchase the leased property for $ ________ until ____________________ (date).

15. *Exercise of Option.* The tenant must notify the owner in writing during the option period if he or she decides to exercise the option.

If the tenant exercises the option, the owner agrees to sign the attached contract of sale. (Attach a contract of sale form with all of the blanks filled in.) Tenant will be given credit toward purchase price for ____% of the rent paid.

AGREED TO:

____

OWNER

____

BUYER

5

Home Improvements

In these inflationary times, building a home addition often makes more sense than buying a larger home. But home improvements often run into messy problems, and precautions are justified. You should enter into home improvement contracts, such as Form 19, with caution, making sure that the contractor is reputable. A contract is no more valuable than the parties entering into it.

One client of ours was having a swimming pool installed in his backyard. During construction a retaining wall collapsed. The pool company refused to repair the wall. All work stopped until the homeowner hired another company to rebuild the wall at a cost of about $1,000. This problem could have been avoided by providing for it in the contract. Paragraph 6 of Form 19 states that the contractor is responsible for damage to the owner's property. If the contractor refuses to agree to this provision because he believes that a wall may collapse, the damage provision can be changed, but be aware of the risks involved.

Theft of building materials is very common. Work sites cannot be guarded around the clock. Make sure that you provide for the theft of materials, making either the contractor or the owner responsible.

Progress payments are very common in home improvement contracts. Do not provide for too large an initial down payment. The initial down payment usually should be about equal to the cost of materials or about 25 to 35 percent of the total cost of the job.

Price the materials yourself. If you are putting in an extra bathroom, price all of the plumbing fixtures that you can. Builder's costs are about 25 to 40 percent off the list price. You can estimate how much the plumber is adding for labor.

You can agree to pay a worker for materials plus an hourly amount. This is riskier than a fixed-price contract, but often a contractor will estimate that a job will take longer than it actually does.

Be Aware of Subcontractors

The homeowner can get caught between the contractor and a subcontractor and be squeezed into bankruptcy. A typical example is as follows: A homeowner signs an agreement with a general contractor to build a den on his home. The general contractor hires three subcontractors, who do all the work. The contractor hires a plumber, an electrician, and a carpenter. You pay the contractor in full and all the work is completed properly. The contractor skips town without paying the plumber, the electrician, and the carpenter.

Next you get notices in the mail that the subcontractors have filed a lien (or claim) against your house because they haven't been paid. Every state has a type of mechanic's or workman's lien. This means that if a worker improves your home by adding pipes or wiring or plaster or paint, and he doesn't get paid, he has a claim against your home. If you don't pay the worker to get the lien removed (or released), your home could be subject to a foreclosure sale. When a home improvement contract has been completed, each contractor and subcontractor should sign a release of lien when the final payment is made.

To protect yourself against this nightmare, you can do several things. First, make certain that any contractor you deal with is duly licensed in your city and/or state. Second, make sure that the contractor is bonded. A bond will provide for payment of claims against the contractor even if he skips town. Third, check out references of the contractor, look at other work that he has done, and find out how long he has been in the business. Finally, try to get the contractor to agree to give you the right to veto subcontractors. If he agrees, carefully check out the subcontractors. See Form 19, Paragraph 10.

You can be the general contractor yourself. You can hire the drywall person, the painter, and the carpenter. It will take a great deal of your time, but you should be able to save money. Since you will pay each contractor yourself, you don't have to worry about workers' liens.

Worker's Compensation Insurance

Whether you are the general contractor or you hire one, worker's compensation insurance must be provided. Worker's compensation, an insurance policy that pays workers for on-the-job injuries, is required in most states. If a worker is injured while repairing your home, you may be sued for his injuries, so make sure that the contractor has worker's compensation coverage.

Progress Payments

Workers want to be paid as they go along. Contracts will usually provide that they get paid in stages. Take a bathroom, for example. Let's say that the bathroom remodeling costs are a total of $1,500. If the materials cost $500, a $500 deposit on signing the contract would be reasonable. The following payment schedule would be fair:

Event	Amount of Payment
Signing contract	200.00
Removal of old tub, sink, and toilet	250.00
Installation of new tile	250.00
Installation of new tub, sink, and toilet	300.00
Painting and completion	$500.00
Total payments	$1,500.00

If The Contractor Walks Away

Contractors have been known to abandon projects because they underbid them and are losing money. They may have hired a subcontractor because he gave them the lowest bid, but the subcontractor decided to abandon the job. When the general contractor walks away from the job, it is time to call your lawyer.

Adjustments to Contracts

Nearly every construction job involves additions and deletions. You decide that you really want the expensive Italian floor tile instead of the tiles from Taiwan that you had decided on. Barring any family arguments, this should not be a problem; any contract that is made can be amended. You should list all the changes in writing and have the contractor sign them. The changes should reflect the price increases or deductions as follows:

Amendment to Contract

The owner and the contractor agree to the following changes in their contract signed on the _______ day of _________________, 19____.

Changes:

Substitute Italian B903 tile for floor

Use old sink faucet

Price

Add $100 to total

Deduct $25

Total increase $75

Agreed to: ______________________________
OWNER

____
CONTRACTOR/DATE

Conclusion

Even if you draft a home improvement agreement, it is worthwhile to have an attorney review it, as this will buy you some peace of mind. A half-hour consultation with an attorney may cost you up to $50, but it is like buying an insurance policy.

If you sign a home improvement contract, make sure that you have checked out the background of the contractor, that the subcontractors have been paid, and that the contractor carries workmen's compensation insurance and is fully bonded and licensed. After you have checked all of these things, cross your fingers and pray that the roof doesn't cave in during construction.

Form 19

Home Improvement Agreement

1. *Parties.* This agreement is entered into between ______________________ (owner) and ______________________ (contractor).

2. *Date of Agreement.* This agreement is made this ____ day of ______________, 19____.

3. *Scope of Work.* The contractor shall provide the following work: ____.

The contractor shall provide the following materials: ______________ ____.

The ______________________________ shall secure all necessary building permits and licenses.

4. *Time of Commencement and Completion.* The work to be done under this contract will be started ________________, and subject to authorized adjustments, completion shall be achieved not later than ________________. If the contractor fails to complete work by ________________, he/she shall pay the owner the sum of $ ________ per day, as liquidated damages, for each and every day that the completion is late.

5. *Contract Sum.* The owner agrees to pay the contractor in cash, certified check, or money order for the performance of the work, subject to additions and deductions agreed to by both the owner and the contractor, the contract sum of $ ________. The contract sum is determined as follows: ______________________________
(Specify how sum was determined.)

PAGE ONE APPROVAL:

______________________ OWNER

______________________ CONTRACTOR

6. *Damage to Property.* The contractor is responsible for any damages caused by his workers. The contractor agrees to repair any part of the home or yard that is damaged.

7. *Theft of Materials.* The contractor is responsible for theft of materials from the work site.

8. *Worker's Compensation Insurance.* The ______________________________ will provide worker's compensation insurance with the ______________________________ ______________________________ insurance company.

9. *Bonding.* The contractor has a bond for $ ________ with the ______________________________ company. A copy of that bond is attached to this form.

10. *Approval of Subcontractors.* The owner has the right to disapprove of the use of any subcontractor. The contractor shall submit the names of all subcontractors for the owner's approval prior to hiring them.

11. *Progress Payments.* The owner agrees to make progress payments on account of the contract sum to the contractor as follows:

Event	*Amount of Payment*
______________________________	________
______________________________	________
______________________________	________

12. *Interest.* Payment due and unpaid under the contract will bear interest from the date that the payment is due at ____% per year.

PAGE TWO APPROVAL:

____
OWNER

____
CONTRACTOR

13. *Termination.* Owner has the right to terminate this agreement if the work performed is not satisfactory.

14. *Final Payment.* Final payment, constituting the entire unpaid balance of the contract sum, will be paid by the owner to the contractor when the work has been completed and the contract fully performed and after the contractor and all subcontractors sign a release of the mechanics' liens. This agreement is entered into as of the day and year written in Paragraph 2 above.

AGREED TO:

____
OWNER

____
CONTRACTOR

Form 20

Release of Liens

The following contractors and subcontractors have furnished materials and labor for the contraction of

____

(describe work completed)

at

____

(address, lot, block, and square)

and have agreed to release all liens for the above-described work.

Date	Name of Contractor and/or Subcontractor	Signature
______	______________________________	__________
______	______________________________	__________
______	______________________________	__________
______	______________________________	__________
______	______________________________	__________

6

Your Job

The average working American earns more than $500,000 in a lifetime. While union members are covered by contracts, most other workers are not. Most people would not think of buying a new car for $5,000 without a contract, and yet they are not covered by a contract in their employment.

The following actual case illustrates the importance of an employment contract. A large New York company hired Mr. R to work in its Washington office. After lengthy negotiations it was agreed that Mr. R would receive $25,000 in salary, and that he would be flown down to Washington to find an apartment. The company agreed that his moving expenses would be paid for and that the company would pay Mr. R's expenses to return to New York if things did not work out in the Washington office. As things turned out, Mr. R was fired in Washington and the company refused to pay any expenses for Mr. R to return to New York. Naturally, there was no written contract. Mr. R has sued for reimbursement of expenses and his loss due to breach of the verbal contract. This case has been in court for well over a year and will very likely remain there for a few more years. If the company and Mr. R had had a written employment contract, their rights and obligations would have been clear. Both parties would have saved on legal fees and the matter would not be tied up in the courts.

Nonunion employees can enter into individual employment contracts with their employers by using Form 21. It includes provisions for salary, commissions, vacation, health and illness benefits and termination. As the example above illustrates, you should include any other terms that are agreed upon between the employee and the employer.

This contract is for the benefit of both the employer and the employee, neither of whom wants to spend valuable business time in court. If your employer has not already suggested an employment contract, he should respect your business sense for suggesting a written contract.

Form 21

Employment Contract

1. *Parties to Contract.* This contract is made between ______________________________ (employer) and ______________________ ______________________________ (employee).

2. *Date of Contract.* This employment contract is effective ________________________.

3. *Base Salary.* The employer shall pay the employee $ __________ per year, payable in equal installments on the first and fifteenth days of each month.

4. *Commission.* The employee shall be entitled to a commission based on the following: ____
____
____.

5. *Vacation.* The employee shall be entitled to ___ days of paid vacation per year.

6. *Health and Sick Leave Benefits.* The employee shall be entitled to the following health and sick leave benefits:
____

7. *Other Benefits.* ____
____

8. *Termination.* Either party may terminate this agreement on not less than ___ days' notice.

AGREED TO:

____
EMPLOYER DATE

____
EMPLOYEE DATE

7

Taking Care of Business

You are interested in starting your own business. Before opening your doors to the public you should consult with a lawyer and an accountant in your area. This chapter will not take the place of a lawyer, but it will provide you with a basic understanding of types of business organizations. There are four basic types of business organizations:

1. sole proprietorship
2. partnership
3. limited partnership
4. corporation

These organizations have different filing requirements. Forms must be filed with state agencies to form limited partnerships and corporations. Tax forms and business licenses must be filed for every business. The four types of business organizations are taxed differently. Your lawyer and accountant can advise you concerning the best form for your needs and for your tax bracket.

Sole Proprietorship

A sole proprietor is simply an individual who starts a business by himself. The sole proprietor usually is required to obtain business licenses in his local area. In addition, he is usually required to obtain worker's compensation insurance for his employees. The individual proprietor must file sales tax forms, pay unemployment compensation to both the state and federal governments and file a Schedule C (Profit or Loss from Business or Profession) with his federal and state income tax forms.

Some states require sole proprietors who use a name for their business, such as Dominique's Restaurant, to register the fictitious name of the business. Because requirements like this vary from jurisdiction to jurisdiction, you should consult with a lawyer in your community.

Partnerships

A partnership is like a marriage. Some are good; some are bad. Some partners are unfaithful. Some are "old faithful." Choose your partner(s) as carefully as you would choose a wife or husband.

A partnership is a business owned and run by two or more individuals who intend to make a profit. All partners in a partnership are liable for all debts and other liabilities of the partnership. If your partner buys 5,000 Greek vases on credit for the partnership gift shop, you are fully liable to pay for the vases. It doesn't matter that your partner did not consult you first.

If you and someone else are equal partners, each of you must declare as income (or deduct as loss) one-half of the partnership income. The partnership is required to file an informational return with the IRS (currently Form 1065). Each partner must file a Schedule E (Supplemental Income) reporting his share of the profits or losses of the business.

The partners have unlimited liability for debts of the partnership. In other words, if you put $1,000 into a partnership, you stand to lose the $1,000 plus everything else that you own if the partnership goes deeply into debt or is sued for something else. Therefore, do not form partnerships too easily. Investigate the options available: limited partnerships and corporations.

Partnership agreements, such as Form 22, create liability and agency relationships between the partners, which may make you liable for the actions of your partner. Enter into partnerships only with individuals you know exceedingly well and trust thoroughly. If you decide to form a partnership, put your agreement into writing. And once again, consult your attorney and accountant!

Limited Partnership

A limited partnership is a partnership formed by two or more individuals, with at least one general partner and at least one limited partner. A general partner is fully liable for the debts of the partnership. A limited partner is liable only to the extent of his investment.

Limited partners are similar to shareholders of a corporation because their liability is limited. General partners are similar to partners in a conventional partnership because their liability is unlimited.

Limited partnerships are not permitted in all states. In states that do permit them, a certificate must be filed with the appropriate state officials. Consult a lawyer in your community regarding these procedures.

Corporations

A corporation is a separate legal entity, separate from its shareholders. All corporations issue shares of stock. The shareholders are not liable for the debts of the corporation. This is one of the major advantages of corporations.

In most jurisdictions in order to form a corporation, articles of incorporation must be filed with the secretary of state or other state officer. The proper forms vary from state to state. Write to the officials of your state for the forms, filing fees, and other information. A complete list of the appropriate state officers can be found in Appendix A, located at the end of the book. If you prepare the articles of incorporation yourself, it is advisable to have an attorney review them before filing them.

Professional Corporations

In many states professionals such as doctors, dentists, and lawyers can incorporate themselves and become professional corporations. *Beware:* each state has its own professional corporation requirements; an accountant or architect may be allowed to incorporate in one state and not in another. Also, certain professionals, such as writers, cannot incorporate in most states. Thus, a lawyer should always be consulted concerning a decision to form a professional corporation.

TO INCORPORATE OR NOT TO INCORPORATE: WHY SHOULD A PROFESSIONAL INCORPORATE?

The pluses and minuses of forming a professional corporation can fill textbooks. These advantages and disadvantages primarily vary according to your tax bracket.

The Disadvantages: Professional corporations are separate entities from the professionals in the corporation. The corporation, like all corporations, must file and pay federal, state, and local income taxes. The professional corporation, or PC, is required to file annual fees to the state or district in which it is incorporated. The PC and its employees pay higher Social Security taxes than professional partnerships.

Malpractice insurance rates are often higher for corporations than for partnerships. The PC becomes subject to unemployment taxes and worker's compensation for its professional employees.

More accounting and legal fees are usually incurred by professional corporations than partnerships because of the additional forms and taxes that have to be prepared and filed. These are the most glaring disadvantages of a professional corporation.

The Advantages: Nearly all of the positive elements concerning a professional corporation are tax advantages. The pension and profit sharing laws favor the corporation, some say unfairly.

The PC can pay for, and deduct for tax purposes, certain payments that a partnership cannot. The PC can purchase health and life insurance for its employees, or it can pay for medical expenses of its employees and deduct these payments from the corporation's gross income.

Tax rates for corporations are often lower than individual tax rates. The professional corporation can retain surplus income and may be allowed to loan this surplus to its officers or employees at little or no interest. The Internal Revenue Service questions this practice, but so far the U.S. Tax Court has ruled in favor of taxpayers on this issue.

A professional corporation enjoys limited liability, similar to any other corporation. But a professional is always liable for his own wrongful or negligent acts. In a PC, if one doctor commits medical malpractice, only he, and not others in the corporation, can be sued. The shares of ownership of a professional corporation are easier to transfer than shares in a partnership.

Other Factors: A professional in a PC does not have to pay estimated income taxes. His taxes are withheld by the corporation and deposited with the U.S. Treasury. This may be an advantage or a disadvantage, depending on whether the problems associated with paying estimated taxes outweigh the disadvantages of getting net income payments.

Again, consult with an attorney who is knowledgeable in the area of professional corporations before you make a decision concerning incorporating.

Stockholders Agreements

One drawback to a corporation is that the small shareholders can be squeezed by the large stockholders. Corporations are controlled by the board of directors of the corporation. These directors are elected by the shareholders. Each share of stock gets one vote. Therefore, the owner of a majority of the stock can control the board of directors and thus control the corporation.

To protect minority shareholders it is possible to provide them with certain rights. These rights can be spelled out in the articles of incorporation, or they can be provided for in a stockholders agreement. In a small corporation, agreements among the shareholders concerning exercise of their voting and other rights are very common. These stockholders agreements, such as Form 23, can prevent future disputes among the owners of small corporations. The effect of agreements like these varies from state to state. Consult with an attorney in your community before approving a stockholders agreement.

Subchapter S Corporation

You may have heard someone mention the *subchapter S corporation.* Subchapter S refers to that subchapter of the Internal Revenue Code. A subchapter S corporation has limited liability like any ordinary corporation but is taxed like a partnership. It is used for small corporations with ten or fewer stockholders. Ask your accountant if this form of corporation could save you some tax dollars.

Conclusion

Creating a business is a serious and risky venture. Be cautious. Seek the advice of individuals with knowledge of the type of business that you want to set up. Plan your steps carefully. Consult an accountant and an attorney in your area before you make a serious business commitment.

Partnership Agreement

1. *Name.* The name of the partnership is ______________________

2. *Partners.* The names of the partners are ____________________

____.

3. *Place of Business.* The principal place of business of the partnership is located at ______________________________________

4. *Nature of Business.* The partnership shall engage in the following business: ____

____

____.

5. *Duration.* The partnership shall commence business on ______ ____________________ (date) and shall continue until terminated by this agreement.

6. *Contribution of Capital.* The partners shall contribute capital in proportionate shares as follows:

Partner	Share
____________________	____________________
____________________	____________________
____________________	____________________

PAGE ONE APPROVAL:

____

____

7. *Allocation of Depreciation or Gain or Loss on Contributed Property*. The partners understand that, for income tax purposes, the partnership's adjusted basis of some of the contributed property differs from fair market value at which the property was accepted by the partnership. However, the partners intend that the general allocation rule stated in Section 704 (c)(1) of the Internal Revenue Code of 1954 shall apply, and that the depreciation or gain or loss arising with respect to this property shall be allocated proportionately between the partners, as allocated in Paragraph 5 above, in determining the taxable income or loss of the partnership and the distributive share of each partner, in the same manner as if such property had been purchased by the partnership at a cost equal to the adjusted tax basis.

8. *Capital Accounts*. An individual capital account shall be maintained for each partner. The capital of each partner shall consist of his original contribution of capital, as described in Paragraph 5, and increased by additional capital contributions and decreased by distributions in reduction of partnership capital and reduced by his share of partnership losses, if these losses are charged to the capital accounts.

9. *Drawing Accounts*. An individual drawing account shall be maintained for each partner. All withdrawals by a partner shall be charged to his drawing account. Withdrawals shall be limited to amounts unanimously agreed to by the partners.

10. *Salaries*. No partner shall receive any salary for services rendered to the partnership.

PAGE TWO APPROVAL:

____________________ ____________________

11. *Loans by Partners.* If both partners consent, one of them may lend money to the partnership at a rate agreed on by both partners in writing, at the time any loan is made.

12. *Profits and Losses.* The net profits of the partnership shall be divided proportionately between the partners, and the net losses shall be borne proportionately as follows:

____

____

____

____ .

13. *Management.* The partners shall have equal rights in the management of the partnership.

14. *Books of Accounts.* The partnership shall maintain adequate accounting records. All books, records, and accounts of the partnership shall be open at all times to inspection by all partners.

15. *Accounting Basis.* The books of account shall be kept on a cash basis.

16. *Fiscal Year.* The books of account shall be kept on a fiscal year basis, commencing January 1 and ending December 31, and shall be closed and balanced at the end of each year.

17. *Annual Audit.* The books of account shall be audited as of the close of each fiscal year by an accountant chosen by the partners.

PAGE THREE APPROVAL:

____

____

18. *Banking.* All funds of the partnership shall be deposited in the name of the partnership into a checking or savings account as designated by the partners. Checks shall be drawn on the partnership account for partnership purposes only. Both partners shall be authorized to sign checks. Any purchase of over $ ________ must be authorized by both partners unless exigent circumstances preclude such authorization.

19. *Retirement.* Any partner may retire from the partnership upon sixty days' prior notice to the other partner. A retiring partner shall be entitled to the then existing weekly draw for ________ weeks from the date of his notice of termination.

20. *Death or Insanity.* The death or insanity of a partner shall cause an immediate dissolution of the partnership.

21. *Election of Remaining Partner to Continue Business.* In the event of the retirement, death, or insanity of a partner, the remaining partner shall have the right to continue the business of the partnership, either by himself or in conjunction with any other person or persons he may select, but he shall pay to the retiring partner, or to the legal representatives of the deceased or insane partner, the value of his interest in the partnership in addition to the weekly draw for ________ weeks, as described in Paragraph 18.

22. *Valuation of Partner's Interest.* The value of the interest of a retiring, deceased, or insane partner shall be the sum of (a) the partner's capital account, (b) any unpaid loans due the partner, and (c) the partner's proportionate share of the accrued net profits remaining undistributed in his drawing account. No value for goodwill shall be included in determining the value of a partner's interest.

PAGE FOUR APPROVAL:

________________________________ ________________________________

23. *Payment of Purchase Price.* The value of the partner's interest shall be paid without interest to the retiring partner, or to the legal representative of the deceased or insane partner, in three monthly installments, commencing on the first day of the second month after the effective date of the purchase.

24. *Termination.* In the event that the remaining partner does not elect to purchase the interest of the retiring, deceased, or insane partner, or in the event the partners mutually agree to dissolve the partnership, the partnership shall terminate and the partners shall proceed with reasonable promptness to liquidate the business of the partnership. The assets of the partnership shall first be used to pay or provide for all debts of the partnership. Thereafter, all money remaining undistributed in the drawing accounts shall be paid to the partners. Then the remaining assets shall be divided proportionately as follows:

____

____

____

____

____ .

AGREED TO:

____
DATE

____
DATE

Stockholders' Agreement

1. *Parties to Agreement.* The following individuals are stockholders of ______________________ corporation and are parties to this agreement:

____

____

____.

2. *Date of Agreement.*

____.

3. *Officers and Directors.*

a. As stockholders of the corporation the parties agree to vote all of their stock for the election of the following directors of the corporation:

____

____

____.

b. As directors of the corporation the parties agree to vote or direct their designees to vote for the following officers:

Name	Position

c. The parties agree that a unanimous vote shall be required for all decisions of the board of directors.

PAGE ONE APPROVAL:

____

____

4. *Sale of Stock.* The parties agree that any sale of stock must be first offered to the parties to this agreement on a proportional basis. Any attempted sale in violation of this provision is void.

A stockholder desiring to sell his or her stock in the corporation shall provide notice in writing of his or her intention with the other parties to this agreement, stating the terms of the proposed sale. The other stockholder shall have ____ days to purchase these shares, on a proportional basis, at the specified terms. If these terms are not accepted by any or all of the other stockholders, they shall be considered to have waived their right of first refusal and the stockholder who has given notice shall be at liberty to sell the shares to anyone on the same terms as provided in the notice.

5. *Salaries of Officers and Directors.* The salaries of the officers and directors of the corporation shall be as follows:

Name	Annual Salary
______________________________	______________
______________________________	______________
______________________________	______________
______________________________	______________

6. *Duration of Agreement.* This agreement shall continue in force as long as all of us or our heirs own stock in the corporation. This agreement shall be binding on our heirs.

AGREED TO:

____
DATE

____
DATE

____
DATE

8

Borrowing Money

"It takes money to make money." Borrowing money is usually necessary to start a business, buy a car, or make investments. Whenever you borrow or lend money you are entering into a contract. There are generally two types of loan agreements. Loans are either secured loans or unsecured loans.

A secured loan means that the borrower has guaranteed payment of the loan with property, which is known as collateral. The secured property can be sold by the lender if the borrower fails to repay the loan.

The most common example of a secured loan is an automobile loan. The bank or finance company has security interest in the car and can repossess the car if payments are not made on time.

A security agreement must be signed for any secured loan. Form 25 is a security agreement, which ties the commitment to repay to a tangible piece of property, such as real estate or an automobile. If the loan is not paid according to its terms, the property can be sold to pay off the loan through repossession or foreclosure proceedings.

In a security agreement the borrower conveys an interest in a property (an automobile, for example) to the lender. The lender holds an interest in the car until the loan is paid back. Both the lender and the borrower are protected by the security agreement: the borrower cannot sell the car during the loan period, and the lender cannot wrongly assert ownership over the vehicle.

This agreement must be filed with a government office in order to be effective. Your attorney or a local bank can tell you the proper place for filing security agreements in your area.

Two agreements are necessary for a secured loan: the loan agreement and the security agreement. Form 25 is a security agreement.

The second type of loan is an unsecured loan. In this arrangement there is no collateral; the lender is said to make a personal loan. When you charge something on your credit card or when the bank gives you a line of credit, you are usually getting an unsecured loan.

Loan agreements, such as Form 24, are useful for purposes other than insuring that the loan will be repaid. As between relatives, or between a corporation and a director of the corporation, a loan can prove to the Internal Revenue Service that money was the proceeds of a loan rather than taxable income or a taxable gift. This form provides for security for the loan in paragraph nine. If you want to make an unsecured loan, this paragraph should be stricken. Except for that one paragraph, a secured loan and an unsecured loan are identical.

An unsecured loan is often held by a promissory note. A promissory note represents a simple loan transaction and can be used when an amount of money is to be repaid fully in one payment at a specific date or when the loan is to be paid back in installments, plus interest, on specific dates. A promissory note, such as Form 26, is documentary proof of a loan and usually specifies the terms and conditions for repayment.

The difference between a secured loan and a simple promissory note is this: If a secured loan is broken, the remedy is built into the agreement. The borrower forfeits the security that he has put up. However, if a promissory note is breached, the lender must sue the borrower and hope that the borrower has sufficient assets to pay the debt. Some examples will illustrate the difference between the secured loan and the promissory note:

Mr. Q borrows money from the bank to buy a new VW Rabbit. The bank holds the title to the Rabbit until the loan is paid. If Mr. Q fails to repay the loan, then the bank can repossess the car and sell it to pay the money that Mr. Q owes the bank. If Mr. Q pays the loan in full, the bank will give the title of the car back to him; Mr. Q now owns his car outright, so he hops into his Rabbit and drives happily away.

Now take the example of Mr. X, who borrows $1,000 from Ms. Y so he can buy a used MG. Mr. X signs a promissory note in which he agrees to pay $100 on the fifteenth day of each month until the balance is paid. After two months Mr. X slyly stops payments on the money due on the promissory note. If she wants her money back, Ms. Y must now sue Mr. X for the amount of money owed. She will have to sue for breach of contract and most likely go through lengthy court proceedings to obtain her money.

At this point it should also be noted what would happen in these cases if the borrower declared bankruptcy. In the case of Mr. Q and the bank, the bank would still be able to sell the Rabbit and thus collect its money. However, Ms. Y's hands would probably be tied, as she would have no priority and would probably collect nothing.

Whether you obtain a secured or unsecured loan depends on your circumstances. If you have a good credit rating and a lot of assets, you are more likely to be given an unsecured loan; this is probably more beneficial to the borrower because it means that his property is not tied up with the lender and can be sold without any interference.

What happens if the borrower has a secured loan in which the bank holds the title to his Ski Nautique, for example, and he wants to sell it? The borrower would go to the bank, saying that he wanted to sell the boat. The bank would agree to release the title upon receiving a full payment of the amount due on the loan. The borrower would receive money from a purchaser, pay off the bank, and give the purchaser the title to the boat. Consequently, everyone involved should be happy.

Form 24 is a detailed loan agreement. It contains many of the provisions that have been discussed above. A prepayment clause states that the borrower may pay the entire balance prior to the day it is due without being charged the full finance charge. Some lenders may say that you must pay the full finance charge, even if you repay your loan early. Do not agree to such a condition. You should not be penalized for repaying your debt early.

The loan agreement also contains a provision entitled "co-borrowers." If you are borrowing money along with another individual or with a group of people, make sure that all names appear on the contract so that everyone will be equally responsible and equally liable. This is important. In one case one of our clients borrowed a sum of money with a group of people. Our client signed the promissory note himself, and the group used the money for business purposes. The group was then unable to pay the loan, and the bank consequently sued the signer of the note—our unhappy client. He in turn had to sue the rest of the group, who were equally responsible but had not signed the note. Had all of the people involved in the loan signed the promissory note, this situation would have been avoided.

Finally, the forms in this chapter can be used privately if you are lending money to someone or borrowing money from an individual. We recommend, if you are borrowing money from a bank, that you suggest that they use your form. If the bank refuses, have them spell out their form in plain English. Make sure that you understand the agreement completely before you sign it.

Form 24

Loan Agreement

1. *Parties.* The words I and me mean

________________________________, the borrower who signed this agreement. The lender is ________________________________.

2. *Date of Agreement.* ______________________.

3. *Promise to Pay.* ___ months from today, I promise to pay to lender ____________________________ ($ ________).

4. *Responsibility.* Although this agreement may be signed below by more than one person, I understand that we are each as individuals responsible for paying back the full amount.

5. *Breakdown of Loan.* This is what I will pay:

1. Amount of loan: $ ________
2. Other (describe): $ ________
3. Amount financed: $ ________
   (Add 1 and 2)
4. Finance charge: $ ________
5. Total of payments: $ ________
   (Add 3 and 4)

Annual percentage rate: ________%

6. Repayment. This is how I will repay:

I will repay the amount of this note in ___ equal uninterrupted monthly installments of $ ________ each on the ___ day of each month starting on the ___ day of __________________, 19___, and ending on __________________, 19___.

PAGE ONE APPROVAL:

________________________________ ________________________________

BORROWER LENDER

7. *Prepayment.* I have the right to prepay the whole outstanding amount at any time. If I do, or if this loan is refinanced—that is, replaced by a new note—you will refund the unearned finance charge, figured by the rule of 78—a commonly used formula for figuring rebates on installment loans.

8. *Late Charge.* Any installment not paid within ten days of its due date shall be subject to a late charge of 5% of the payment, not to exceed $ ________ for any such late installment.

9. *Security.* To protect lender, I give what is known as a security interest in my auto and/or other: (Describe) ______________________

____ .

10. *Default.* If for any reason I fail to make any payment on time, I shall be in default. The lender can then demand immediate payment of the entire remaining unpaid balance of this loan, without giving anyone further notice. If I have not paid the full amount of the loan when the final payment is due, the lender will charge me interest on the unpaid balance at ____ percent (%) per year.

11. *Right of Offset.* If this loan becomes past due, the lender will have the right to pay this loan from any deposit or security I have with this lender without telling me ahead of time. Even if the lender gives me an extension of time to pay this loan, I still must repay the entire loan.

12. *Collection Fees.* If this note is placed with an attorney for collection, then I agree to pay an attorney's fee of fifteen percent (15%) of the unpaid balance. This fee will be added to the unpaid balance of the loan.

13. *Co-borrowers.* If I am signing this agreement as a co-borrower, I agree to be equally responsible with the borrower for this loan.

AGREED TO:

______________________________ ______________________________

BORROWER LENDER

Form 25

Security Agreement

1. *Parties to Agreement.* This agreement is entered into between ______________________________ (borrower) and ______________________________ (lender).

2. *Date of Agreement.* ________________________.

3. *Security Interest.* The borrower conveys to the lender a lien and security interest in the following vehicle:

Manufacturer: ______________________________

Model: ______________________________

Year: ______________________________

Type of Body: ______________________________

Serial Number: ______________________________

The security interest and lien include all additions and improvements to this vehicle.

4. *Termination of Agreement.* This agreement terminates when a promissory note for $ __________, dated ________________________, between the borrower and lender is paid in full.

5. *Possession of Vehicle.* The borrower is entitled to maintain possession of the secured vehicle until the borrower fails to make timely payments on the promissory note described in Paragraph 4.

6. *Condition of Vehicle.* Borrower agrees to maintain the vehicle in good condition, agrees to keep the vehicle free of claims for taxes and repairs and agrees not to misuse the vehicle. Borrower agrees to use the vehicle strictly according to the laws of the state where it is driven.

PAGE ONE APPROVAL:

______________________________ ______________________________

7. *Insurance.* Borrower agrees to insure the vehicle against fire, theft, and collision in the amount of $ ____________________, and to provide lender with evidence that the insurance was obtained.

8. *Repossession of Vehicle.* If any payment on the promissory note described in Paragraph 4 is more than ten days late, the lender is entitled to possession of the vehicle. Before taking possession of the vehicle, the lender is required to notify the borrower by certified mail that the lender intends to repossess the vehicle.

The lender may repossess the vehicle only by nonviolent means. If the borrower refuses to peaceably give up possession of the vehicle, the borrower may seek a court order requiring the borrower to give up possession. In the event that a court order to relinquish possession is necessary, the lender is entitled to recover reasonable attorney's fees.

9. *Address Changes.* The borrower agrees to inform the lender within ten days of any change of address.

10. *Notarization.* ____________________, borrower, appeared before me, this ____ day of ____________________, 19____, and signed this agreement.

AGREED TO:

____
SIGNATURE OF BORROWER

____
SIGNATURE OF LENDER

____
NOTARY PUBLIC

WARNING: THIS AGREEMENT MUST BE RECORDED OR FILED WITH APPROPRIATE GOVERNMENT OFFICIALS IN YOUR JURISDICTION, SUCH AS THE RECORDER OF DEEDS OR THE REGISTRAR OF TITLES. CHECK TO MAKE SURE THAT YOU FILE A COPY OF THIS AGREEMENT IN THE PROPER GOVERNMENT OFFICE(S).

Form 26

Promissory Note

$ ________ ____________________ (city)

____________________, 19____.

On or before ____________________ (date), for value received, I promise to pay ____________________ (lender) the sum of ______________________________ dollars ($ ________), with ____% interest.

I agree to make monthly payments on the ____ day of each month for ____ months of $ ________.

____
BORROWER

9

Being in Two Places at Once

Isn't it impossible to be in two places at the same time? No. For example, if you are on a vacation in Alaska and you need to make a withdrawal from your savings account in New York, a power of attorney will allow you to be in both places at the same time. A power of attorney is a legal document that allows another person to act on your behalf. There are two basic types of power of attorney: limited and unlimited.

Unlimited Power of Attorney

An unlimited power of attorney, such as Form 27, gives another person the right to act in your place for all purposes and gives that person the power to sell your property and commit you to other obligations. In order to give someone this tremendous power, you must trust him or her very much.

If you are planning to be out of the country for a year or so it may be advisable to confer a power of attorney on your sister or brother or someone else you trust.

Limited Power of Attorney

Form 28 is a limited power of attorney that allows another person to act in your place only for specified purposes. If you have a car in California and you are in Nebraska, you can give a limited power of attorney to a friend so that he can sell your car for you.

We suggest that you issue a limited power of attorney whenever possible because you do not want someone to have more authority to act in your affairs than he may actually need. This can lead to abuse of the power of attorney. Also, insert a fixed date or time period by which the power of attorney will expire. You can always execute another power of attorney, so don't give more time than is necessary.

When you revoke the power of attorney, do so in writing and notify all parties involved that you no longer authorize anyone to act in your behalf. In this way you will avoid the problem of someone making commitments on your behalf against your wishes.

Form 27

Unlimited Power of Attorney

____________________________ provides

____________________________ full power of attorney on this ____ day of ______________________, 19____. ____________________________ shall have the power and the right to sell or assign my real and personal property, to enter into contracts in my name, to withdraw funds from bank and savings accounts in my name, to use my property as he chooses, to enter my safe deposit boxes as he chooses and to do any and all acts as I could do personally.

This power of attorney shall be valid until revoked by me. I retain the power to revoke it at any time.

I fully understand the contents of this document and fully trust ____________________________ to act in my best interests.

In accepting this power of attorney ____________________________ agrees to act in good faith and in the best interests of ____________________________.

I accept this power of attorney.

____

Subscribed and sworn to before me this ____ day of ______________________, 19____.

____
NOTARY PUBLIC

Signed in the presence of the following witnesses:

____
WITNESS (SIGNATURE) (PRINT NAME)

____
ADDRESS OF ABOVE WITNESS

____
WITNESS (SIGNATURE) (PRINT NAME)

____
ADDRESS OF ABOVE WITNESS

____

Form 28

Limited Power of Attorney

______________________________ provides

______________________________ limited power of attorney on this ____

day of ________________________, 19____, and

______________________________ shall have the right to:

____

____ .

This limited power of attorney will be valid until it is revoked by me. I retain the power to revoke it at any time.

I fully understand the contents of this document and fully trust ______________________________ to act in my best interests.

In accepting this limited power of attorney ______________________________ agrees to act in good faith and in the best interests of ______________________________.

I accept this limited power of attorney.

____

Subscribed and sworn to before me this ____ day of

________________________, 19____.

____

NOTARY PUBLIC

Signed in the presence of the following witnesses:

____

WITNESS (SIGNATURE) (PRINT NAME)

____

ADDRESS OF ABOVE WITNESS

____

WITNESS (SIGNATURE) (PRINT NAME)

____

ADDRESS OF ABOVE WITNESS

10

Writers, Artists, and Inventors

We discussed real property and personal property in earlier chapters. A third kind of property is known as creative property. Creative property includes fiction, nonfiction, plays, screenplays, poetry, lyrics, music, visual arts (such as films, photographs, paintings, sculpture, etc.), inventions, and all other original ideas.

Artists and writers generally tend to ignore the noncreative or business side of their craft because of the time and distractions involved. Consequently, creative people are vulnerable to exploitation.

Robert Indiana, a well-known visual artist, learned the hard way that he had to protect his creative property. He is best known for his LOVE prints. In the early 1970s, reproductions of his work as sculpture, jewelry, prints, and coffee mugs were widely available. Millions of dollars were made on these unauthorized reproductions and, because Indiana failed to copyright his creative property, he lost millions.

Copyrights

A copyright is the right to own creative property, such as literary works; musical works; pictorial, graphic, and sculptural works; motion pictures and sound recordings, as recognized and sanctioned by law. A copyright entitles the holder to the exclusive right to own, prepare, and produce copies of the work, and to distribute, perform, display, and sell copies of the literary, musical, or artistic work.

Copyright protection can be obtained by placing a copyright notice on every work of art, music, or literature that you produce. This notice consists of placing the letter C in a circle or the word *Copyright*, followed by the name of the copyright holder and the year of the first publication of the work. For example, if David Lee wrote an original novel in 1980 and wished to protect it by copyright, he would place the following notice on one of the first pages of the manuscript or published book:

©1980 by David Lee
or
Copyright 1980 by David Lee

Phonograph records and other sound recordings are protected by placing the letter P in a circle, followed by the year and the name of the holder of the copyright:

℗1981 by David Lee

The notice should be place prominently so as to give reasonable notice to anyone obtaining a copy. In a book, for example, the notice is usually placed on the back of the title page.

The appearance of the notice alone is sufficient to establish and protect your rights; however, if there is an infringement of those rights, you must register your copyright with the U.S. Copyright Office in order to bring suit in a federal court. This is a matter of procedure and can be done at any time before filing your lawsuit.

The copyright notice also provides international protection, since the United States is a member of the Universal Copyright Convention, to which many countries belong.

You cannot copyright an idea. The idea must be reduced to concrete form, such as writing, pictures, or models. The more specific and tangible the form, the better. In no case does copyright protection for an original work of authorship extend to any idea, procedure, process, system, method of operation, concept, principle, or discovery, regardless of the form in which it is described, explained, illustrated, or embodied in such work.

Registration of Copyright

Four registration forms cover all manner of creative work: SR (Sound Recording), VA (Visual Arts), PA (Performing Arts), and TX (Nondramatic Text). These may be obtained by writing to: Copyright Office, Library of Congress, Washington, DC 20559. When requesting your registration form, be specific as to the type of work you wish to copyright.

In registering publishable work or sound recordings, one copy of the work should be sent with your application and fee ($10), if it is a prepublication registration. Application for copyright after publication should be done within three months following publication of the work and two copies of the best printed edition should be sent to the copyright office. The U.S. Government becomes the sole owner of these copies, and they become part of the collection of the Library of Congress.

After your application has been processed, you will receive a Certificate of Registration containing the information given in your application, along with the registration number and effective dates of the registration. (Copyright protection, registered or unregistered, is for the owner's lifetime, plus fifty years.) If for some reason the Register of Copyrights determines that the material deposited is not copyrightable, you must be notified in writing of the reasons for refusal.

Patents and Trademarks

Patents and trademarks are more costly and more difficult to obtain than copyrights. You will know when a company has a trademark: its product is marked ™, for trademark, or ® for registered trademark.

The names of products are protected by trademarks, such as Coca-Cola, TM, the Coca-Cola Corporation.

Patents are the exclusive right to use and manufacture inventions. They are very expensive to obtain. We recommend that you consult a patent attorney for advice concerning your invention. The only recognized specialty for lawyers is patent law; these attorneys must pass an examination before they can be listed as patent specialists.

Trademarks are easier to obtain than patents, but we do not recommend that you file applications for trademarks without consulting an attorney. We have seen too many mistakes made by nonlawyers who attempted to obtain a registered trademark and failed. The trademark office occasionally loses applications, so they must be closely watched.

Consignments of Art

You are a struggling young artist. The tenth gallery that you go to offers to put your work on display on consignment, which means that you leave the work in the possession of the gallery, but you still own it. When the artwork is sold, you get your share of the proceeds, usually two-thirds.

A consignment agreement, such as Form 29, gives an art gallery or store the right to sell your artwork or other items, and requires that store or gallery to pay you a percentage of the sale after the sale has been transacted. Make sure that you get a copy of a written consignment agreement before leaving the artwork. Do not trust the gallery; art galleries often go out of business.

When an art gallery goes bankrupt, the artwork that is on consignment may be auctioned along with the artwork that the gallery paid for. The artist will be treated as any other creditor of the gallery; this means that the artist will be paid only a small percentage of what he or she is owed. Protect yourself by putting a bankruptcy provision into the consignment agreement.

Form 24 is a consignment agreement that contains a bankruptcy clause. Under this provision, if the art gallery does not pay when the art is sold or goes bankrupt, the artist has a claim, or lien, for the artwork. This means that the artist still owns the work, and the person who bought it must satisfy the debt owed to the artist, or the artist has a right to reclaim the work.

Warning: To preserve the artist's claim or lien, the consignment agreement must be filed with the governmental office in the gallery's area that files security agreements. If you don't know where this office is, you will have to consult with a lawyer. A local bank should be able to provide this information.

Consignments are risky, but the galleries may not be willing to pay you directly for your work. Consignments out of town are particularly risky since you cannot easily check on the gallery. Be careful to keep a close watch on galleries where you leave works on consignment; make sure they display the works properly.

Conclusion

Your creative property may be your most valuable possession. Protect it wisely. Above all, protect yourself by getting copies of consignment agreements and keep copies of all copyright, patent, and trademark applications filed for your creations.

Copyright Registration Form*

For Original Registration

Form TX: for published and unpublished nondramatic literary works

Form PA: for published and unpublished works or the performing arts (musical and dramatic works, pantomimes and choreographic works, motion pictures and other audiovisual works)

Form VA: for published and unpublished works of the visual arts (pictorial, graphic, and sculptural works)

Form SR: for published and unpublished sound recordings

For Renewal Registration

Form RE: for claims to renewal copyright in works copyrighted under the old law

For Corrections and Amplifications

Form CA: for supplementary registration to correct or amplify information given in the U.S. Copyright Office record of an earlier registration

Other Forms for Special Purposes

Form GR/CP: an adjunct application to be used for registration of a group of contributions to periodicals in addition to an application Form TX, PA, or VA

Form IS: request for issuance of an import statement under the manufacturing provisions of the Copyright Act.

For more detailed information about all these forms, write for Circular R1c.

Application forms are supplied by the U.S. Copyright Office free of charge. *Photocopies of application forms are not acceptable for registration.*

There is no requirement that applications be prepared or filed by an attorney.

Reprinted from Circular R1 Copyright Basics distributed by the U.S. Copyright Office, Library of Congress, Washington DC 20559 (September 1980).

Consignment Agreement

1. *Parties to Agreement.* ______________________________ (gallery), ____ (address) has received the following works of art from ______________________________ (artist) who lives at ____.

2. *Artwork.* The works of art included in this consignment agreement are:

____, retail price $ _________;
____, retail price $ _________;
____, retail price $ _________.

3. *Date.* This agreement is entered into this ____ day of ________________________, 19____.

4. *Commission.* The retail price of the artwork listed above minus the gallery's commission of ____% shall be sent to the artist within ten days of sale.

5. *Title to Artwork.* Title to the artworks, and a lien and security interest in the artworks and in any proceeds from their sale, is reserved by the artist until the proceeds are sent to the artist.

6. *Rights of Artist.* In the event that the gallery does not send the artist payment within ten days after sale, or if the gallery becomes bankrupt, the artist shall have all rights of a secured party under the Uniform Commercial Code.

PAGE ONE APPROVAL:

____

____

7. *Insurance.* The gallery shall be responsible for the loss or damage of the above-described artwork and shall be insured for this purpose.

8. *Termination of Agreement.* At any time prior to sale of the artwork the artist has a right to request delivery of it, but the artist shall be responsible for paying shipping and mailing charges. The gallery has the right to terminate this agreement by returning the artwork to the artist.

AGREED TO:

____

GALLERY

____

ARTIST

WARNING: ARTIST SHOULD RECORD THIS AGREEMENT WITH APPROPRIATE GOVERNMENT OFFICIALS; SEE CHAPTER 9.

11

Wills

"Do you really think I need a will? I would really rather talk about it later." This is the general reaction of most people when they are confronted with the fact that they should have a written will. Because of the connection with death, people are often afraid to speak about wills and generally try to avoid the subject.

A will is a written orderly disposition of one's property that takes effect after his or her death. If an individual dies leaving a will, he is said to die *testate*. Barring unforeseen challenges, the wishes of the deceased, expressed in the will, are carried out.

If an individual dies without a will, he is said to die *intestate*. In this situation the distribution of property is decided by the state. In other words, if a person dies intestate his personal choice is taken away and that of the state of his residence is imposed.

We have several recommendations concerning wills. First, you should have an attorney write your will for you. It is relatively inexpensive to have a will written by an attorney, and it is not particularly time consuming. Before visiting a lawyer you should decide for yourself how you would like your property distributed. Keep in mind that the law will generally not permit you to disinherit or exclude your spouse from your will, even if you specifically attempt to do so. The law will usually give your spouse one-third to one-half of your estate. You can generally disinherit other individuals, however.

The law on wills varies greatly from state to state on such issues as the number of witnesses, signing procedures, and other technical requirements. A local attorney can answer your questions regarding these matters very inexpensively. We estimate that, if you decide how you want to dispose of your property before seeing an attorney, and upon seeing him have a *simple* will written, it should cost you between $60 and $200. Obviously, this will vary from state to state.

How should you prepare to see an attorney? Make a list of all your property, real estate, personal effects, savings and checking accounts, and any other property that you own. You can then decide who you would like to receive the various items. Take the list with you when you go to the lawyer's office. You can have a will written in which you direct that all of your property be sold and that the money be distributed among people whom you designate. You can leave a particular piece of property to a particular individual. The possibilities are endless, so make your decisions, then see an attorney, and you will save a lot of money.

Many people say, "I only have a couple of relatives, so I don't really need a will." What can happen if you don't have a will? As already explained, each state has laws that provide for the distribution of property of individuals who have not taken the step of having a will drawn up. And, more likely than not, the state will distribute the property in a way that would not be particularly pleasing to you. Have a will made, if you haven't already; then your property will not be subject to an arbitrary distribution but will go where you specify in your will.

A simple will, such as Form 30, disposes of your property after your death. The individual who makes this will leaves all of her real estate as well as 50 percent of any money in the bank to her husband. She also leaves specific pieces of property to her daughter and son. If you wish to leave specific pieces of property to an individual, be sure to describe that item carefully in your will. Do not leave room for mistakes. Be sure to account for all property you wish to specifically leave to someone.

Paragraph six of the will directs that all property not previously mentioned should be sold and that the proceeds should be divided among the children. This is a residual clause that covers all property not already left to someone. Without this paragraph, the individual may have left property for which no provision was made. Even if you think that you have covered all of your property, you should include a paragraph similar to this to avoid inadvertently omitting any property.

The second paragraph appoints an executor and trustee of your will. This individual will be responsible for paying all the debts of your estate and distributing the property of the estate. You can give this individual broad power to decide whether he will give specific items to individuals or sell everything, or you can limit his power to do only as you direct by your will. In this form the executor is directed to sell everything and give the money to the children. He has no discretion.

The power you bestow on the executor is up to you; however, we suggest that you be as specific as possible when making your will so that your wishes are carried out.

Last Will and Testament of

I, ______________________________, of the city of

___________________, and state of ________________, being of sound mind, memory, and understanding, declare this to be my last will and testament, as follows:

1. *Debts and Funeral Expenses.* I direct that all debts enforceable against my estate, and funeral expenses, be paid as soon as possible.

2. *Executor and Trustee.* I nominate and appoint ______________________________ as executor and trustee of my estate. My executor and trustee shall have the full power at his discretion to do all the things necessary for the liquidation of my estate.

3. *Spouse.* I give and bequeath to my ______________________________ (husband or wife) all my interest in real estate and 50% of all money that I have in banks, savings and loans, certificates of deposit, and similar institutions.

4. *Children.* I give and bequeath the following items to my children. To my son, ____________________________, I give ______________________________.

To my daughter, ____________________________, I give ______________________________.

To my ____________, ____________________________, I give ______________________________.

5. *Charity.* I give and bequeath the following items to charitable organizations. To ____________________________, I give ______________________________.

To ______________________________, I give ______________________________.

PAGE ONE APPROVAL:

____

6. *Remainder of Estate.* I direct that the remainder of my estate be sold and that the proceeds be divided as follows:

____

____.

7. *Death of Beneficiaries.* In the event that any of the beneficiaries named in this will die before me, or at approximately the same time as me, I direct that their children shall take their share, equally. In the event that any of the beneficiaries die before me without leaving children, I direct that the remaining named beneficiaries shall take their share, equally.

8. *Revocation of Other Wills.* I hereby revoke all prior wills, codicils, and testamentary dispositions made by me.

IN WITNESS TO THIS WILL I HAVE SET MY HAND TO THIS WILL THIS ___ DAY OF __________________, 19___.

____

This will, consisting of two pages, each bearing the signature of ____________________________, was signed on this date, and declared by ____________________________ to be his last will and testament. The will was signed in the presence of the following three witnesses:

____
WITNESS

____
SIGNATURE

____
ADDRESS

____
WITNESS

____
SIGNATURE

____
ADDRESS

____
WITNESS

____
SIGNATURE

____
ADDRESS

12

Breach of Contract

You have a contract with someone to sell your color TV, but the person fails to bring the $250, as agreed. The buyer has breached the agreement contract. Although this is serious, as well as annoying, not every breach of contract deserves to be made into a federal case.

Arbitration of Disputes

Both parties to a contract can agree to refer disputes to an impartial third person. You may agree that a mutual friend will decide how the dispute will be resolved or that you will refer a dispute to some other objective third party. The sample arbitration clauses that follow can be added to any of the form agreements in this book:

1. *Arbitration of Disputes.* Any controversy or claim arising out of this agreement shall be settled by compulsory arbitration in accordance with the rules of the American Arbitration Association. The arbitrator shall be ______________________ (insert the name of a mutually agreeable person or an arbitrator selected according to the procedures of the American Arbitration Association).

2. *Arbitration of Disputes.* If any dispute arises between us

relating to this agreement, we agree that the dispute may be determined only by an arbitrator selected by the American Arbitration Association. We each relinquish the right to have any other person represent either of us at a hearing before this arbitrator. The arbitrator's decision shall be binding, final, and nonappealable. The arbitrator shall not have the right or the power to award part of his determination of a dispute any expense incurred by either of us relating to the dispute or the hearing before the aribtrator, except the arbitrator's fees and a hearing reporter's fees.

3. *Arbitration of Disputes.* If any dispute arises between us relating to this agreement, we agree that the dispute may be determined only by an arbitrator selected by the American Arbitration Association. We each relinquish any right that we may have to have any other person represent either of us at any hearing before the arbitrator. The arbitrator's decision shall be binding, final, and nonappealable. Both of us shall equally bear the arbitrator's fees.

The preceding arbitration clauses are simple and straightforward. Choose the clause that most fits your needs. The advantage of including an arbitration clause in an agreement is that you may be able to settle the dispute more quickly and efficiently than if you have to go to court.

Small Claims Court

Every city has a small claims court. Claims of varying amounts (usually $1,000 or less) can be filed on simple forms. The clerks of these courts are usually very helpful. Small claims courts were designed to be used by individuals without lawyers. Most lawyers will not take a small claims case because the time expended will usually be too great in relation to the amount of money involved.

Filing fees in small claims courts are usually $5 or less. Often small claims matters come to trial in a matter of weeks, rather than the years that a larger case can take.

Major Disputes

When the contractor refuses to proceed with the construction of your roof and water is still leaking in, ruining your Afghan rug, it's time to call a lawyer. Often a phone call to a lawyer can resolve a dispute or devise a plan of action. When you find out that the odometer in the car you bought has been turned back from 160,000 miles to 60,000 miles, it's time to call an attorney. When your wife leaves you and cleans out your joint checking account, it's time to see a lawyer.

Back to That Color TV

We started this chapter with the breach of the contract for the sale of a color TV. The buyer refuses to pay for the set. You, of course, have not let the TV out of your sight since you haven't been paid. You should try to find another buyer. If you can't find a buyer who is willing to pay the same price, but you find one who will buy the set for $200, your damages will be $50 plus any additional advertising that you may have bought. After you compute your damages, you will have to decide if it is worth the time and effort to go to small claims court.

13

Lawyers

In our world today, matters are becoming increasingly complex, and sometimes it seems as though lawyers are taking over. Throughout this book we encourage the use of contracts to avoid unnecessary legal disputes. However, it is sometimes necessary to seek professional legal assistance when you are entering into a major agreement, such as the purchase of a home. This book does not attempt to teach you how to practice law, nor does it attempt to replace attorneys.

The question of when you need a lawyer is very complex and yet often dictated by common sense. If you are entering into an agreement and you are uncertain of its consequences or ramifications, it is always advisable to consult an attorney *in advance*. Most people wait until they have already involved themselves in complex legal matters, and then they call a lawyer. By checking things out in advance, you can save a lot of money and avoid unnecessary litigation. Many attorneys have a free initial consultation, and at that time you can determine if you really have a legal problem.

Selecting an attorney should not be a difficult matter but should be done with care. Most local bar associations have referral lists of approved attorneys who are qualified to help you. Always ask the attorney if he or she has handled the type of case that you are involved in.

Lawyers are also now permitted to advertise. In most newspapers, attorneys advertise their prices for wills, divorce, bankruptcy, personal injury claims, and other legal matters. It is very easy to compare prices and call to speak with an attorney. Many attorneys who advertise offer either a free or a very minimal initial consultation fee.

When selecting an attorney, ask the same questions that you would if you were hiring anyone else. Inquire about experience, areas of expertise, and get a clear picture of his fees. There are so many different types of law firms that, unless you examine the firm closely, you may find yourself involved with attorneys who are unable to handle your particular problem with the expertise that you should expect.

We have included three simple forms in this chapter: a contingent fee agreement, an hourly fee agreement, and a fixed fee agreement. Law is a profession, but it is also a business. We would encourage you to negotiate with your attorney over his fee if you think it is unreasonable. If he has set fees that are not within your means, he will certainly refer you to another attorney.

An attorney will generally handle a personal injury case, such as an injury resulting from an automobile accident, on a contingent fee basis. Before entering into a contingency fee arrangement an attorney must believe that your case is worth pursuing. A contingency fee agreement, such as Form 31, only awards the attorney a fee if he prevails in the case. This means that the attorney will charge you a percentage of whatever he collects for you. This percentage generally varies from 33 1/3 percent to 50 percent. This is negotiable and should be written on your retainer agreement when you hire your attorney. Under a contingent fee agreement the attorney will get no fee if you do not recover any money. All agreements usually contain a provision that states that the client is responsible for all costs and out-of-pocket expenses; such as the cost of filing suit, service fees, postage, and photocopying. Ask for an estimate of how much the out-of-pocket expenses will be, and then tell your attorney that you want to be informed if the costs go over that amount.

It should be noted here that American Bar Association ethics forbid an attorney to accept any criminal case on a contingent fee basis.

An hourly fee agreement simply means that you retain your attorney for a specified amount of money per hour. Most attorneys base their charges on an hourly fee. When entering into an hourly fee agreement (Form 32), make sure that the attorney agrees to itemize all charges in detail. Ask your attorney how many hours he expects to spend on the matter. No lawyer will be able to tell you the exact amount of time, but be sure to make it clear that you want to be informed periodically of the number of hours that he spends on your case and what he is doing for you. No matter what type of agreement you have with your attorney, make sure that he sends you a copy of all relevant papers.

In a fixed fee agreement the attorney agrees to perform a particular task, such as writing a will or a simple divorce, for example, for a set price. Make sure you know whether this fee includes the costs of the suit as discussed above. Clients will usually appreciate a fixed fee agreement, such as Form 33, since it puts a limit on the expenses that the client will incur for legal work.

Whether you have a contingent fee agreement, an hourly agreement, or a fixed fee agreement, make sure that you have a signed contract before your attorney begins work. Just as in any other contract, make sure that you and your attorney both know your respective rights and responsibilities. This will lead to a healthy and productive client-attorney relationship.

Contingent Retainer and Fee Agreement

1. This is a retainer and fee agreement entered into between
______________________________ (client) and
______________________________ (attorney).

2. Client retains ______________________________ as his attorney to represent him concerning ____
____ .

3. The client agrees to pay attorney ____% of the gross amount collected as compensation for his efforts in pursuing these matters settled before filing in court, or if suit is filed. In addition to this fee percentage, client agrees to pay all out-of-pocket expenses, including court costs, necessary to pursue these claims.

4. In agreeing to Paragraph 3 the client understands and agrees that the fee and costs as stated will constitute a lien upon all monies recovered on the client's behalf.

5. The client understands and agrees that this fee arrangement does not include legal services in connection with the prosecution of this claim on appeal. Client will have the choice to retain attorney under a new fee arrangement should this matter involve appellate litigation.

6. If no recovery is made on client's behalf, there will be no charge for legal services, the fee provided for being contingent upon a recovery, with the exception of out-of-pocket expenses.

7. Attorney agrees to provide client with copies of all relevant documents arising out of this case.

AGREED TO:

__________________________________ __________________________________
CLIENT DATE ATTORNEY DATE

Form 32

Hourly Retainer and Fee Agreement

1. This is a retainer and fee agreement entered into between
____________________ (client) and
____________________ (attorney).

2. Client retains ____________________ as his attorney to represent him concerning ______________________________
______________________________.

3. The client agrees to pay attorney $ ________ per hour for his legal work regarding this matter. Client also agrees to pay for all out-of-pocket expenses, including court costs, photocopying charges, and long-distance phone charges.

4. The client agrees to pay attorney a retainer of $ ________, against which the charges described in Paragraph 3 will be deducted.

5. After the retainer is depleted attorney will bill the client monthly, itemizing all charges. A ____% annual interest charge will be added to all accounts with balances due for more than thirty days.

6. If client disputes any charges, the client must notify attorney within thirty days. Attorney will make every effort to clarify or correct any disputed charge.

7. The client understands and agrees that this fee arrangement does not include legal services in connection with the prosecution of this claim on appeal. Client will have the choice to retain attorney under a new fee arrangement should this matter involve appellate litigation.

8. Attorney agrees to provide client with copies of all relevant documents arising out of this case.

AGREED TO:

____________________ ____________________
CLIENT DATE ATTORNEY DATE

Form 33

Fixed or Flat Retainer and Fee Agreement

1. This is a retainer and fee agreement entered into between

_______________ (client) and

_______________ (attorney).

2. Client retains _______________ as his attorney to represent him concerning _______________

_______________.

3. The client agrees to pay attorney $ ___ for his legal work regarding this matter. Client also agrees to pay for all out-of-pocket expenses, including court costs, photocopying charges, and long-distance phone charges.

4. The client agrees to pay attorney a retainer of $ ___, against which the charges described in Paragraph 3 will be deducted.

5. The client understands and agrees that this fee arrangement does not include legal services in connection with the prosecution of this claim on appeal. Client will have the choice to retain attorney under a new fee arrangement should this matter involve appellate litigation.

6. Attorney agrees to provide client with copies of all relevant documents arising out of this case.

AGREED TO:

____
CLIENT DATE

____
ATTORNEY DATE

14

Conclusion

The primary goal of this book is the prevention of legal problems. Before you enter into any new legal arrangements we suggest that you review the relevant chapters of this book. While this book will not answer all of your legal questions, it should provide you with basic legal knowledge; you should now have enough knowledge to be able to ask the right questions.

If you have learned the following basic principles, you have already begun to prevent legal problems:

1. Get a copy of everything that you sign.
2. Read and understand every agreement that you sign.
3. Put all of your agreements into clear, concise written form.
4. Make sure that everything you buy is in acceptable mechanical condition; hire a professional to write a written report on the condition of the house or vehicle that you are considering buying.
5. Writers and artists: put a copyright notice on your work.
6. Consult with an attorney even when you are writing your own agreements; often preliminary consultation is free or very low in cost.

Appendix A State Officers

State	*Filing*
Alabama	Secretary of State Montgomery, AL 36100
Alaska	Commissioner of Commerce Juneau, AK 99801
Arizona	Corporation Commission Phoenix, AZ 85000
Arkansas	Secretary of State Little Rock, AR 72200
California	Secretary of State Sacramento, CA 95801
Colorado	Secretary of State Denver, CO 80200
Connecticut	Secretary of State Hartford, CT 06100
Delaware	Secretary of State Delaware Corp. Division Dover, DE 19901

State	*Filing*
District of Columbia	Office of Superintendant of Corporations 6th and D Streets, NW Washington, DC 20001
Florida	Secretary of State Tallahassee, FL 32301
Georgia	Secretary of State Atlanta, GA 30300
Hawaii	State Treasurer Honolulu, HI 96800
Idaho	Secretary of State Boise, ID 83700
Illinois	Secretary of State Springfield, IL 62700
Indiana	Secretary of State Indianapolis, IN 46200
Iowa	Secretary of State Des Moines, IA 50300
Kansas	Secretary of State Topeka, KS 66600
Kentucky	Secretary of State Frankfort, KY 40601
Louisiana	Secretary of State Baton Rouge, LA 70800
Maine	Secretary of State Augusta, ME 04301
Maryland	Maryland State Charter Department Baltimore, MD 21201
Massachusetts	Secretary of the Commonwealth Boston, MA 02100
Michigan	Department of the Treasury Corporation Division Lansing, MI 48904

State	*Filing*
Minnesota	Secretary of State St. Paul, MN 55100
Mississippi	Secretary of State Jackson, MS 39200
Missouri	Secretary of State Jefferson City, MO 65101
Montana	Secretary of State Helena, MT 59601
Nebraska	Secretary of State Lincoln, NE 68500
Nevada	Secretary of State Carson City, NV 89701
New Hampshire	Secretary of State Concord, NH 03301
New Jersey	Secretary of State Trenton, NJ 08600
New Mexico	State Corporation Commission Santa Fe, NM 87501
New York	Secretary of State Albany, NY 12200
North Carolina	Secretary of State Raleigh, NC 27600
North Dakota	Secretary of State Bismarck, ND 58501
Ohio	Secretary of State Columbus, OH 43200
Oklahoma	Secretary of State Oklahoma City, OK 73100
Oregon	Corporation Commissioner Salem, OR 97301

State	*Filing*
Pennsylvania	Department of State Harrisburg, PA 17101
Puerto Rico	Secretary of State PO Box 3271 San Juan, PR 00904
Rhode Island	Secretary of State Providence, RI 02900
South Carolina	Secretary of State Columbia, SC 29201
South Dakota	Secretary of State Pierre, SD 57501
Tennessee	Secretary of State Nashville, TN 37200
Texas	Secretary of State Austin, TX 78700
Utah	Secretary of State Salt Lake City, UT 84100
Vermont	Secretary of State Montpelier, VT 05601
Virginia	State Corportion Commission Richmond, VA 23200
Washington	Secretary of State Olympia, WA 98501
West Virginia	Secretary of State Charleston, WV 25300
Wisconsin	Secretary of State Madison, WI 53700
Wyoming	Secretary of State Cheyenne, WY 82001

Appendix B Glossary

Acceptance- the act of agreeing to a given offer; when you accept an offer, you bind yourself to taking it in exchange for the item or service in question.

Agreement- synonymous with contract; a mutually accepted arrangement between two or more parties involving the exchange of items, money, or services.

As is- referring to the condition of property to be sold or leased; generally pertains to a disclaimer of liability; property sold in *as is* condition is generally not guaranteed.

Bill of sale- a receipt for purchase of personal property, usually a motor vehicle.

Bond- a written promise of surety to pay a sum of money if the bonded party does not perform specified duties.

Bonded- secured by a bond.

Closing- the transactions that transfer title to property, such as signing deeds and mortgages, and paying for the property.

Co-borrowers- partners in borrowing funds; they can have equal or disparate shares in the loan but have an equal responsibility to pay back the loan. One co-borrower can be sued for the full amount of a loan.

Consideration- something of value, such as goods, services, or money, that is put up as an offer or as acceptance of a contract.

Contingent contract- a contract that provides for the possibility of its termination when a specified occurrence takes place or does not take place.

Contingency- dependent on the fulfillment of a condition that is not yet certain.

Contract- an agreement between two or more persons for the performance of a specified task, or for an exchange of goods or services mutually agreed on; *see agreement.*

Co-signers- parties to a loan agreement who indicate their mutual responsibility for repayment of a loan. One co-signer can be sued for the full amount of the loan.

Exclusive listing- a real estate term; in an exclusive listing arrangement the property is listed with only one broker who will receive a commission if the home is sold during his exclusive listing period, unless it is sold directly by the homeowner.

Exclusive right of sale- a real estate arrangement in which a broker receives a commission whenever the home is sold during the listing period, even when the home is sold directly by the owner.

Fixtures- property that is physically attached to real property, such as plumbing and electrical fixtures.

Fraud- the intentional misleading of a person that causes that person to be financially damaged.

Intestate- when a person dies without having a will he dies intestate.

Lease- a contract that provides for the renting of real estate, cars, or any other type of property.

Liability- money or debts owed; legal responsibility for a claim.

Lien- the legal right to hold or place a claim on property and to have that property sold if the underlying claim is not paid.

Mechanical warranty- a guarantee for a specified time period to repair defects in property; an assurance that the property will be in working order for a certain period.

Mechanic's lien- the lien that a worker has on property for repairs made to that property; for example, an automobile mechanic has a lien on a car that he has repaired, and a plumber has a lien on a home where he installed plumbing.

Offer- the proposal or extension of something of value in exchange for something else; in connection with a contract, usually the offer is one of money in exchange for goods or services.

Open listing- in real estate, this occurs when a homeowner lists his property for sale with more than one real estate agent; the first agent to find a buyer receives the commission.

Option to purchase- in real estate, the right given by the owner to another person to purchase a specific piece of property; an option to purchase personal property can be created.

Personal property- personal possessions, excluding real estate, such as cars, stock, bonds, jewelry, artwork, and furniture.

Priority- the right to precedence in obtaining payment, especially when there is a foreclosure or bankruptcy. For example, a first mortgage on a home has a priority over a second mortgage on that home if the buyer defaults on the loans.

Progress payments- payments made in stages, as services are provided.

Real estate or real property- land or buildings connected to land, including houses, apartment buildings, and condominiums.

Settlement- the time when property legally changes hands; all money is paid and documents signed at the settlement or closing.

Subcontractor- a person or business who contracts to provide work necessary for the performance of someone else's contract.

Testate- when a person dies with a will he dies testate.

Warranty- *see mechanical warranty and warranty of title.*

Warranty of Title- guarantee of legal ownership and rightful possession.

Will- a written declaration of a person's wishes as to the disposition of his property after death.

Worker's Compensation Insurance- an insurance policy, required in most states, that pays workers for on-the-job injuries.